A 2ND HELPING OF CHICKEN SOUP FOR THE INDIAN SOUL

101 More Stories to Open the Heart and Rekindle the Spirit

Jack Canfield
Mark Victor Hansen
Raksha Bharadia

westland

We would like to acknowledge the following publishers and individuals for permission to reprint the following material. (Note: the stories that were penned anonymously, that are in public domain or were written by Raksha Bharadia are not included in this listing.)

All the Right Moves. Reprinted by permission of Smriti Lamech. © 2009 Smriti Lamech.

Being There. Reprinted by permission of Anil Agarwal. © 2009 Anil Agarwal.

Caring for the Spirit. Reprinted by permission of Monika Pant. © 2009 Monika Pant.

(Continued on page 310)

westland ltd
Venkat Towers, 165, P. H. Road, Opp. Maduravoyal Municipal Office, Chennai 600 095
No. 38/10 (New No.5), Raghava Nagar, New Timber Yard Layout, Bangalore 560 026
Survey No. A - 9, II Floor, Moula Ali Industrial Area, Moula Ali, Hyderabad 500 040
Plot No 102, Marol Coop Ind Estate, Marol, Andheri East, Mumbai 400 059
47 Brij Mohan Road, Daryaganj, New Delhi 110 002

Copyright © 2010 Chicken Soup for the Soul Publishing LLC

All rights reserved

10 9 8 7 6 5 4 3 2 1

ISBN 978-93-80283-40-1

This edition is published under arrangement with Chicken Soup for the Soul Publishing LLC, its logos and marks are trademarks of Chicken Soup for the Soul Publishing LLC

This edition is for sale in India, Pakistan, Bangladesh, Nepal and Sri Lanka only

Cover design by design on u

Inside book formatting and typesetting by SŪRYA, New Delhi

Printed at Shri Krishna Printers, Noida

This book is sold subject to the condition that it shall not by way of trade or otherwise, be lent, resold, hired out, circulated, and no reproduction in any form, in whole or in part (except for brief quotations in critical articles or reviews) may be made without written permission of the publishers.

A 2ND HELPING OF CHICKEN SOUP FOR THE INDIAN SOUL

Contents

Introduction ix

1. POWER OF LOVE

All the Right Moves *Smriti Lamech* 2
Being There *Anil Agarwal* 5
Caring for the Spirit *Monika Pant* 7
Dear M *Meenakshi Roy* 10
Dowry *Ramendra Kumar* 14
Forgiveness *Mahesh Dattani* 19
His Bumper Sticker Reads, 'Princess on Board' *Monisha Sen* 21
How Will You Know When It Is for Real? *Upreet Dhaliwal* 23
If Mom Had Been Around *Anusha Parthasarathy* 27
Meeting Kamla *Sangeetha Parthasarthy* 30
Not So Ordinary *Nikhil Kulkarni* 35
Overcoming an Addiction *Huta Raval* 37
Power *Malavika Thiagaraja* 39
The Art of Admonition *Pesi Padshah* 40
The Captain and I *Mahendra Waghela* 43
The Cheesy Romance That Wasn't *Rayna Talwar* 46
The Cheque *Sheetal Goel* 49
The Divinity of Unconditional Love *Shriyaa Trivedi* 54
The Poker Room *Shashi Agarwal* 56
The Wisdom Tooth *Puja Madan* 59
United *Sudesna Ghosh* 62
Writing for Chicken Soup *Seema Agarwal* 64

2. OVERCOMING OBSTACLES

A Different Plane *S. Meera* 68
Bird's Eye *Raksha Bharadia* 71
Fighting Myself *Kabir Singh Bhandari* 74
Following My Footsteps *Sayli Deshmukh* 78
Going to the Roots *Rajan Mishra (As told to Amita Dalal)* 80
Just a Little Patience *Rayna Talwar* 83
Lessons from a Parking Lot Attendant *Komal Venkataraman* 85
Losing the Battle to Win the War *Christina Daniels* 87
My Recollections of Mountaineering *Gunit Locham* 90
Sight Beyond Vision *Piyush Panwar* 94
The Edge *Alaka Yeravadekar* 97
The Indomitable Soldier *Mita Banerjee* 98
The Moment You Wish ... *Rajan Saajan Mishra* 102
   (As told to Amita Dalal)
The Next Best Thing *Suparnaa Chadda* 104

3. BE THE CHANGE

A Glimmer of Hope *Shabbir Merchant* 108
A Hundred and Twenty-Five Rupees *H.P. Singh* 111
Be a Troubleshooter *Sunil Handa* 113
David *Raksha Bharadia* 116
The Deal *Sunil Handa* 119
My Little Step *Heena Patel* 122
One Life *Dimple Ranpara* 124
The Dignity of Labour *Anonymous* 127
The Finger Bowl *Sreelata Menon* 130
The King of Kings *Bhagyashree Sowani* 135
The Principles of Justice and Humanity *Vrunda Thakkar* 138
True Greatness *Rayna Talwar* 140
Working for People *Lakshmi Madhusoodanan* 142

4. A NEW LEASE

A Messiah in Malaysia *Dipika Mukherjee* 146
A Second Chance *Suparnaa Chadda* 149
A Second Innings *Anu Chopra* 153
Fine Line *Heartcrossings* 156
One Rainy Day in Mumbai *Sandhya Krishnan* 158
Requiem for Love *Dhruv Katoch* 161

CONTENTS

Science Versus Spirituality *Suparnaa Chadda* 165
Someone *Amreeta Sen* 167
Superannuation *Chitra Vashisht* 171
Tarot *Divyaa Kummar* 173
The Clear Voice *Janki Vasant* 177
The Open Ground of Middle Age *Jane Bhandari* 181
The White Hair *Ankur Garg* 182
When My Heart Gave Up *Sangeetha Narayan* 184

5. GIVE AND GROW

A Little Love to Spare *Anjana Jha* 188
Angels Don't Always Have Wings *Max Babi* 192
Assignment *Avantika Debnath* 194
Blood Donation *Rehana Ali* 197
Clapping for God *Beryl Kunjavu* 199
For the Tsunami *Manjushree Abhinav* 201
Forgotten Names *Arijit Ghosh* 203
From a Teacher's Desk *Rehana Ali* 206
Moment of Clarity *Manjushree Abhinav* 208
Music of a Stolen Symphony *Nipun Mehta* 210
Reach Out and Help Someone *Ruma Purkayashta* 213
Small Things with Great Love *L.K. Baweja* 215
The Gift of Sight *Vijayalakshmi Ramachandran* 217
The Scooty Ride *Rana Siddiqui Zaman* 219
The Stuffed Toy *Raksha Bharadia* 221
The Volunteer *Priya Pathiyan* 224
Vocal in Times of Beauty *Pavi Mehta* 228

6. A MATTER OF PERSPECTIVE

A Carnation by Any Other Name *Namratha Kumar* 232
Appu *Revathi Seshadri* 234
It Happens Only in India *S. Meera* 238
Lost in London *Ameet Surana* 242
My Hero *Rehana Ali* 245
Of Dal-Chawal and Biryani *Akanksha* 247
On the Birth of My Nephew *Raamesh Gowri Raghavan* 250
Still Indian After Two Hundred Years, Two Oceans, ... 252
Three Continents and Thousands of Miles of Separation
  Shivana Naidoo

The Green Salwar Kameez, Bindi and Bangles *Janki Vasant* 255
The Oil Canvas *Neelam Kothari* 258
Underestimating John *Anu Chopra* 260
What Is Bigger, Destiny or Karma? *Raksha Bharadia* 262
Wrong Side of Thirty-Five! *Suparnaa Chadda* 264

7. THE SPIRIT LIVES ON
Daddy Comes Home *Shankar Hemmady* 268
Fighting for Karuna's Dignity *Rehana Ali* 271
Five Airline Toffees *Natasha Ramarathnam* 274
Lessons from Life *Sandhya Sitaram* 276
October *Suneetha B.* 281
The Blue Sweater *Anupama Kondayya* 285
The Chair *Deepak Morris* 288
Vini *Col. Popli (As told to Vandana Tewari Yadav)* 290

More Chicken Soup? 295
Contributors 297
Permissions 310

Introduction

We were standing in line for a ride in a theme park in Malaysia. It was the 'Tower of Terror'—a hundred-foot vertical drop. As it got closer to it being our turn, I began losing my nerve. The shrieks and screams from those on the ride sent shock waves through me and I begged my husband and kids to let me leave from the side gates. But they called me 'chicken-heart' and insisted that I stay. Willy-nilly, I found myself proceeding with the line when I noticed another 'chicken' ahead of me. She too was pleading with her group, but to no avail. Our eyes met a couple of times and we acknowledged the other's plight; at that moment, it seemed we understood each other better than our closest kith did. Just then, the entry gate opened; it was her turn to sit on the ride. She had the option of leaving, but she went ahead and sat on the ride and then gestured to me that it would be okay.

Interestingly, no other assurance mattered. I too went and sat on the ride, fearful, yet with a kind of courage—the contagion worked! As I stepped down after the ride, a feeling of triumph swept over me. I had conquered a huge fear.

The people we meet, the books we read, the movies we watch, the company we keep, have a bearing. Consciously or subconsciously, they make us, steering our everyday choices and beliefs in one direction or another.

A 2nd Helping of Chicken Soup for the Indian Soul is not just interesting company, with its collection of real-life, humorous, inspiring and stirring tales, it is not just a peek into the private moments of our contributing authors, it is also a wand, a flute that will lead you to memories of your key experiences, happy and unhappy ones. You will find yourself celebrating your relations, victories and strengths (do not forget to share them with us!) and ruminate over disappointments and failings. Most importantly, you will consider possible resolves through our stories.

One of our contributors wrote that, in the process of writing for *Chicken Soup for the Indian Romantic Soul*, she actually journeyed through all the years spent with her husband and realised how supportive and caring he has been throughout, and in the matters she considered central. 'This journey dwarfed my quotidian grudges against him,' she said over G-chat one day.

Each of us has our Achilles heel. Forget about admitting it to others, we often live life without acknowledging it to our own selves! We go to lengths to cover our flaws, prove ourselves bigger, better, by pushing others down either directly or through more tacit means. But such 'wrongs' create inner conflicts and they cannot be bottled easily. Conflicts are never pleasant to deal with, inner conflicts are still tougher to face.

In this compilation, you will read confessions of 'wrongs' owned up to and eventually set right. Our contributors speak candidly of how they gave into their fears and insecurities and how they eventually triumphed over it. They speak of the power of hope and faith even in the face of heavy odds. They speak of second chances, second innings and that life indeed offers opportunities, only that we are not open enough to receive them. As they say, many times we are so engrossed grieving over a shut door that we miss the myriad others that have opened even if they are staring us in our face. This book will help you see openings through a hundred different stories.

Conversations today are rife with how insensitive and selfish the world we live in has turned, we speak at length of our misfortunes and the thoughtlessness of others, yet in the write-ups that I received, I saw the other side—our loving and caring side. I received stories of kindness and compassion from complete strangers, of generosity and forgiveness from the most improbable quarters, and of unconditional love and understanding from loved ones, which we don't see because we have taken them for granted. Every time I read the stories, I recollected incidents where people, at times complete strangers, have stepped out of their comfort zones (when they did not need to) and have cheered me with a kind word, well-meaning advice, much-needed succour or by other sweet means. I remembered the goodness of relatives, friends and colleagues that I did nothing to deserve, yet enjoyed. In the rigmarole of life, I was quick to forget them—reading these stories brought them back. Today I see myself as blessed and loved. You will have difficulty counting your blessings once you are done with this title, dear reader.

We are quick to complain of the rampant corruption in our system and free with criticism of officials, but when it comes to something as simple as standing up against the system, we prefer taking the short-cuts ourselves. I received stories where contributors spoke of their little steps towards handling gigantic issues, and how those steps eventually created a much larger ripple effect. I understood that change starts with me; I saw that, even though I am just one, I am still one and that is enough.

In the end isn't life about 'I matter', 'I am capable' and 'I am loved'? In these stories, you will see that someone up there cares for you too, only that it did not register at the time.

And if you indeed do remember those moments when reading *A 2nd Helping of Chicken Soup for the Indian Soul*, then we have achieved our purpose.

Raksha Bharadia

1
POWER OF LOVE

Love and kindness are never wasted. They always make a difference. They bless the one who receives them, and they bless you, the giver.

—Barbara De Angelis

All the Right Moves

Once in a while, a wedding comes along to remind you of why you got married in the first place. It's particularly useful if it happens to be the seventh year of your own marriage! When waistlines are thickening and attention is thinning. When you're squabbling over who should come home early to help your son learn his lines for a play. When you're annoyed at the other for forgetting an appointment. When you're getting irritated with his habit of dismissing everything you say. When you're angry at her for wasting money you could do with, on bed sheets you could do without. I could go on, but you know what I mean.

It's a beautiful reminder to hear the priest say the familiar lines and say, 'Yes, I do'. I do take this man with his pockmarks, his premature greying and his ugly fingers and toes. Because when I met him I only took in the sharp, perfect features, the warm, brown eyes and the energy surrounding him. And the years do tend to dull things, making you notice only the worst. But then, like silver polish, attending a wedding polishes up the familiar that has dulled with contempt and gives it back its original sheen.

It's only at a wedding that you realise there is no perfect love, but you can aspire to it.

Over the last few years, I've felt a sense of calm. Of

knowing that no matter where we go, I'll be fine. As long as I have my husband with me, I don't feel at sea. He's my home. My anchor. My lighthouse.

So much has gone by in these seven years—word associations only he will get. In jokes. Arguments. And in the midst of all this, when I fight, when I cry over in-law issues, when I shudder at that awful word, 'compromise', a wise friend reminds me of the treasure I found. Of the perfect man I found. Who doesn't share my religion, my community, my customs, my food habits or my language. Yet, is the yin to my yang. Who is fair while I am dark. Who is tall while I am small. Who is easy-going where I am rigid. Who is calm while I am passionate. Who was not offered to me on a platter. Whom I fought tooth and nail to hold on to. Who left behind all his worldly possessions and ties and stood strong, holding my hand. Who loves the tip of my nose. Who thinks my knobbly toes are perfect. Who I picked because he fit me perfectly—not my family or my community.

All these thoughts and more flew around my head like little blue birds, reminding me how I'd struck gold in the husband-finding department. The point was driven home to me, however, when I watched him on the dance floor.

Well, actually, I watched him execute a few twirls and I knew he was itching to get on the dance floor. But he steadfastly stood next to me, his lame (I'd just developed a knee problem!) wife, keeping me company. Until I told him to go dance. With my hot now-a-mommy friend. And then he rushed off to hit the dance floor without a backward glance. It was so cute. But then I saw him dancing and I realised he was good, but not as good as he was in my head. He wasn't burning up the dance floor like he normally did. But I wasn't going to tell him that. He got in a few more dances over the evening and I watched from afar. Proud because he was still the best dancer by miles. But sad that he wasn't as good as he used to be. Was it age? I couldn't accept that. My husband doesn't grow old. He just gets better. ...

And then a favourite number came on and he grabbed me and said, 'You can't sit this out ...' I slipped off my shoes and joined him on a perilous dance floor that had seen a couple of shattered wine glasses that evening. Barefoot, I could just about keep up with the music—but I forgot about my knees.

Know why? Because boy-oh-boy, he was back in business. And I felt awful. I've ruined him! He saves his best steps, his maximum grace and all his enthusiasm for me! Touching though that is, I couldn't help but feel terrible! Here I am, bum knee and all, unable to keep up with even a two-left feet-ed amateur, and yet I am feted, courted and wanted by the real deal!

Is it any wonder that I am still smitten?

Smriti Lamech

Being There

It was 11 January 2004, and I was on my way to Ostrava, a Czech town bordering Poland. This trip was for the business which I had left unfinished in January 2003, when I'd had to rush back to India leaving the business mid-way. This trip was really a compulsion, something which gave me no pleasure.

Heimtex Fair was over; my colleagues were travelling to Amsterdam and I had to travel on alone. I took a flight from Frankfurt to Prague and then boarded the train to Ostrava.

The train chugged out of the station, and as we left the city, you could see the fields and everything covered with snow. The two rail tracks looked like two never-ending lines which do not meet, drawn on white canvas. No life form was seen. Everything looked dead, covered in an endless blanket of snow.

This picture outside was actually a reflection of my feelings within. The whole of last year had been an ordeal, to say the least. My idol, role model, teacher, guide, friend, the most important person in my life, my father, had passed away during that last unfortunate trip of mine, in 2003. It had come as a major blow to me. As I sat there on the train, which seemed to be taking me nowhere, all the memories of last year came rushing back, making me morose and taking me deeper and deeper into a state of sadness. I was feeling lonely and lost.

A whole myriad of emotions were coursing through my mind and body. It was then that my mobile rang. It was Seema, my wife. I gave vent to my emotions as I poured my heart out to her. Guilt at not having been there by his bedside as he left us for good, anger at my helplessness as I could not come back for his last rites, loneliness as I had shared an exquisite relationship with him, and finally my frustration towards life for being so unfair. Last year had been a burden too heavy for my shoulders to bear. But as Seema lent a patient ear with an occasional 'Yes, I know, I understand', I began having a cathartic response. Before I knew it I was feeling rejuvenated and renewed. A pure feeling of being loved engulfed me, soothed and caressed me, till all my emotions were spent.

What had she done? She had just been the shoulder for me to cry on. And it was then I realised the precious gift of life, love. Love is sometimes about just being there. Listening. A comforting presence showing you care. Not always being loud, verbose or expressive. It can be expressed in these little acts which go a long way. . . .

It is amazing how a little effort out of love and care can make such a big difference.

Anil Agarwal

Caring for the Spirit

It was one night in October 2004, when the cyst burst. Excruciating pain, an emergency operation followed by a hysterectomy. Ten days later, the shattering news: the cyst had been malignant and I had to undergo some cycles of chemotherapy.

Does life change overnight? People whom you take for granted assume more importance, issues you consider pivotal to your life become trivial.

People came to visit, and showed concern. In all kinds of ways.

'You'll be alright; you know so-and-so also had this problem ... now look how she has recovered.'

'Just try to bear the pain.'

'You have to be strong you know, for the children.' As if I did not know this. What else was I doing? Why? For my children, of course.

Then again and again those words: 'How are you now?' As if every minute's ordeal had to be chronicled.

'Come on, don't be depressed. Life is difficult; you just have to be strong.'

Words of wisdom, words to fill voids in relationships, gaps in understanding.

The rocks in my life came in the shape of my husband and my two daughters.

Even when tears streamed from my eyes as I sat in the hospital waiting room, he looked away, as if giving me an opportunity to come to terms, knowing that I would have to get my strength from my inner reserves. For he knew that it was the only thing which would make me really strong. He cared for my spirit.

It was his wordless support that gave me so much belief in my own abilities. I would lean back on his shoulder and he would shake me from my stupor and make me live life. Never once did he become my crutch, never once did he allow me to become dependent on him or wallow in self-pity.

My daughters' laughter broke the overpowering spell of chemotherapy. Endless quarrels, just like the old times, teenage tantrums—all these made me believe that nothing had changed. They never made allowances for my illness. They never made me feel that I was anything but normal. They made me fight back better, for they made me believe that I would be alright soon. They protected my spirit.

Then the miracle occurred. Positive energy began to flow from my husband's fingers into my body, from my daughters hugs into my soul.

Every time I would have intravenous chemo drugs administered, my already deep-seated veins would become thinner and more difficult to find. Probing with the needle, the nurse would often have to call for more help. It was then that I realised that my husband had magic in his fingers.

The moment he would touch my forehead, he would just will the pain away. Or perhaps, the touch of his hand would divert my attention to that spot and I would not feel the pain anymore. Thick, oily fluids coursing through my veins and his intense prayers would permeate the very aura around me and infuse me with healing power.

When tossing and turning on my bed at night, he held me tight, as though he would never let me go. And then, the reason for living, the meaning behind the suffering and the thankfulness to my Creator came in a rush. My husband's intense longing for me to be well again gave me the strength to battle it through.

After every overnight stay at the hospital, I would come back home to a cosy room filled with my children's smiles. No flowers, no get-well-soon cards—just smiles, laughter and warmth. When my body reacted strongly to the drugs, I saw mirrored in all the faces around me the worry and consternation. I was choking ... but one look at my family calmed me down—no, I had to overcome it, they could not bear it.

Together we fought the devil of cancer, refusing to accept that it was anything out of the ordinary, by undermining its strength, by refusing to acknowledge its presence, by crushing it with positive energy.

Monika Pant

Dear M

I sat in front of the dresser, draped in white satin, Granny's letter in my hand. I felt calm, collected. Much too calm for a bride, I thought. And then I read the letter again.

15 Sep 2008
Roseville, MN
Dear M,
For the longest time now, you have been asking me to come live with you. Ever since Grandpa left, you thought I would be better off living with family rather than alone. Do you know why I never left? Because your grandpa always came back.

One morning last year, I woke up to a perfect white silence that only a Minnesota winter could bring. And the first thing I saw, cutting through the perfect white, was a set of footprints that trailed away from the door. I walked downstairs to find the couch empty for the first time in a month. His cane was still propped against the couch with his favourite hat hung over it. I picked up the raggedy old Fedora hat and thought of the time I bought it for him. Then I checked all the rooms again, but he was gone. Your grandpa, who could barely walk on his own, had disappeared yet again. It was our forty-second winter together in Minnesota.

I followed the footsteps as far as I could, but as I walked, the falling snow erased them. I stared down the road; my mind obscured by drifting snowflakes and clouded breaths. I wondered if I would ever see him again. I left the door unlocked, in case he came back. I took another look around the house, but I knew he was gone. He had taken off on his own yet again, just like before. And I wondered if he would come back again.

It had been little over a month since the doctor told us there was nothing we could do for him. His organs were failing, a natural part of growing old. I was told to give him a comfortable place to rest. The doctor didn't say how long he had to live, just not long. Ever since, he'd rarely set foot anywhere in the house, aside from the bedroom. And of late, he'd taken to lying around on the couch. He even had his meals there, by himself. And he barely spoke. Whether he was too tired to talk, or was ashamed for being a burden, I can't say. I admit that this made me immensely mad at times. But after he left, although I was used to his sudden unexplained absences over the years, I felt an overwhelming sadness that I never thought was possible. And so, each morning I gazed out of the window and thought back on that day. I wondered if he was still alive. The police found no trace of him. I didn't know if this was good or bad news. At least I could maintain hope that he was still alive. His hat and cane still sat against the couch as a reminder that he did exist after all. But the most difficult part was to convince you and the rest of the family that I would be fine on my own, that Grandpa would come back. He always did.

The winter melted away and the earth was painted green. Every morning I looked out of the window, half expecting him to come back as suddenly as he had disappeared. Spring drifted into summer and still I watched. You thought I was a crazy old woman. But I waited for him. I knew he would be back. And then I had a dream. That I had ensnared a mighty eagle, clipped its wings and caged him for life. There he was, peering out of the cage in helpless anguish, longing to fly and dreaming of the day when he would. And I stood by, watching him silently suffer. I woke up in fear. The fear was not that he would cease to endure. The fear was that he would cease to dream. And I knew right then why Grandpa had to leave. And why he always came back.

Summer slowly faded, autumn fires covered the trees in yellow and red. I watched the last leaf fall off the tree outside my window and thought of the months I had spent alone. I was so focused on the leaf, floating and looping in the air, that at first I did not notice the figure walking up to my door.

By the time I got downstairs your grandpa was already lying down on the couch, just as he should have been all those months ago. He had his Fedora hat tilted forward on his head, covering his eyes. He cocked it up as I entered the room, exposing a single eye. We stared at one another for what couldn't have been as long as it seemed. The questions were choking us, yet he waited for me to ask. I finally asked him where he'd gone and why.

'This city was killing me. There were some things I had to do before it was my time to go.'

'What things? Why leave without saying anything?'

'Just some errands. You were asleep, I didn't want to wake you,' he answered.

'Why did you come back?' I asked, not sure if I was happy or angry to see him. This had been happening for too long now. I was tired.

'Forgot my hat,' he said.

I stared at him, looking for any sign of emotion. But he simply laughed.

'You've always taken things too seriously. I did what I had to do out there. I'm ready to just relax now. Besides, I missed you. I know I haven't been a great husband, but I want you to know that I love you, and I appreciate you being here for me at the end.'

I pressed him for more details, but he dipped his hat back over his eyes and said, 'I'll tell you about it tomorrow, I'm tired.'

He slept through the day, and when I woke up the next morning, I looked out of the window again, forgetting that he was back. I ran downstairs in a panic, only to find him lying still on the couch. In his hand was a piece of paper, folded and tattered. I tried to wake him, but that wasn't happening. He had passed away that night.

I took the paper from his hands, expecting to find a note of some sort. But it wasn't a note, it was a list. The list included exotic places around the globe, Morocco, Sri Lanka, Nepal, and more. There were ridiculous dishes, famous monuments, and people whose names I did not recognise. All the items on the list were crossed out except for one. At the bottom of the list was, 'Say goodbye to wife'. I took a pen and scratched it out, then slipped the list back into his hand. Then I sat back and reflected on the wedding vows I took forty-two years back.

He's gone again, your grandpa. But this time around, he won't be coming back. He took the old Fedora hat with him, you see. My job here is finally done. That's why I'm writing to let you know that I shall be joining you early next month.

Until then, lots of love,
Granny

I folded the letter and placed it back on the dresser. Then I walked out to take my own wedding vows.

Meenakshi Roy

Dowry

It was two weeks to Manasi's fourteenth birthday. She was lying with her head on her father's lap, her eyes closed. He was sitting on the bed with her mother beside him. They thought she was sleeping.

Manasi's father, Jaidev Mishra, was a tall, broad-shouldered man. He sported a thick, long moustache, which he kept twirling whenever he was in a thoughtful mood. He had a booming voice and big, strong hands. Even though he looked tough, at heart he was gentle and sensitive. And one only had to look into his eyes to see the kindness, the warmth that lay behind the rough exterior. Manasi's mother, Chitra, in contrast, was small, petite and sharp-tongued. Manasi was scared of her temper.

'Jaidev, I really think you are spoiling Manasi too much,' Chitra told her husband.

'Don't be silly. Have you been reading too many of those agony aunt columns? No one gets spoilt by love. One only gets destroyed by the lack of it.'

'Whatever you say, your obsession with Manasi is not healthy. I am telling you for your own good!'

'What do you mean, Chitra?' Jaidev demanded.

'She is fourteen. In another ten years or so she will get married. What is going to happen then? How will you stay without her?'

'I've already thought about that. I am going to go with her as part of her dowry. I would be eligible for voluntary retirement by then. I'll take it and go with her. You know Manasi is going to be either a district collector or a senior-ranking IPS officer. Well, when she returns from duty I'll be there waiting for her. I'll open the door of her car smartly and carry her briefcase inside. I'll do odd jobs for her. I'll work as her chauffeur, bodyguard, secretary or assume any other role she wants me to. I'll happily stay in the outhouse of her bungalow. All I want is to be with my little princess.'

He bent down and kissed Manasi softly on her cheek.

'Really Jaidev, you don't take anything seriously,' Chitra chided.

'But I am serious! Whether you come with me or not, I'll go with my Manasi as her dowry,' Jaidev said, gently running his fingers through his daughter's soft, silky hair.

*

It was seven. Papa still hadn't come home. It was her fifteenth birthday and he had promised to be home by six.

Just then the telephone rang. She rushed and picked up the receiver.

'Papa, do you know what the time is?' she started off before Jaidev could even mumble hello.

'Manasi, ma, please don't get angry. I know I'm late. I got stuck in a meeting. My boss is also as difficult to please as you. Please forgive me, ma. I'll be there in ten minutes. I am talking from the bakery. I thought I'd talk to my princess while the cake is being packed. I'll cool her down a bit or she'll put a curse on me and turn me into a toad,' he laughed his booming laugh, which she loved so much.

Manasi couldn't help smiling. It was so difficult to be angry with him. Whenever she was furious with him he would call her 'ma' in that special voice of his and she would simply melt.

At 7.30, the phone rang again. Chitra picked up the receiver.

'Bhabhi, Jugal Patnaik here. There ... there is bad news ...' Jugal Patnaik was Jaidev's colleague in his office.

'Wha ... what happened?'

'Jaidev ... Jaidev has had a heart attack. He is in the ICU of Ispat General Hospital. I have sent the company vehicle. Please come quickly.'

Twenty minutes later they were in the hospital, when they were told that Jaidev had passed away.

They later found out that Jaidev had suffered a stroke in the car on the way home from the bakery. Jugal Patnaik, who was with Jaidev, rushed him to the hospital. In the ICU he suffered another stroke, which proved fatal.

Over the following days, Manasi saw everyone around her weeping. But she hadn't cried. However, she had almost stopped speaking. Every day she would go to Jaidev's tiny little study and stare at his table and his chair for hours together. She would pick up old albums and keep looking at the photographs.

Sometimes she would tell her mother, 'Mama, why don't you make suji halwa today. You know Papa likes it so much.'

'Have you stitched the button on Papa's blue blazer, mama? Winter is coming and he will be wearing it. He looks so handsome in that blazer, much smarter than even Sharukh Khan.'

Chitra tried explaining things to her gently. But she just wouldn't listen.

'No, you are all wrong. Papa is not dead. Papa never goes anywhere without telling me. He might not tell you but he always tells me. He loves me much more than anyone in the world. He is just playing chhuppa-chhuppi with me. He'll soon come out of hiding ...'

Manasi even refused to go to school. 'I want to be there when Papa comes home. If he looks for me and doesn't find me here he will be disappointed.'

Chitra spoke to Dr Sanjeeb Mohanty, their family physician, who advised her to give Manasi time since she was obviously in a state of shock. 'It's important for her to cry,' he said. 'Once she does that, she will gradually get over it.'

A week later, their neighbour came over. Her daughter was getting married and she wanted to show Chitra the purchases they had made for the wedding. Chitra took Manasi along.

They were led straight into the bedroom where everything was laid out for inspection on a huge double bed.

'Wow is this the wedding sari?' another visitor asked, picking up a bright red sari. 'It's terrific. It must have cost a lot.'

'Thirty-two thousand,' Chopra aunty said. 'And you know, Pinky's father has handpicked each and every item. He told me, "Pinky is our only child. I will give her such an exquisite dowry, the whole world will envy it".'

There was a muffled sound and Chitra looked up. Manasi was staring at Chopra aunty, tears flowing down her cheeks. As Chitra reached out, she turned and ran away.

Five minutes later, when Chitra entered Manasi's room, she found her lying face down on the bed. Her whole body was shaking. The pillow was wet with tears. In her hand was a photograph of her father's body on the funeral pyre.

A few days later, Chitra was in the living room, leafing through a magazine, when Manasi came in.

'See what I found in his study.'

Chitra looked at Manasi. In her hand was a cassette.

'I found this cassette. It has a song for me in Papa's own voice. You know what a terrible singer he was and how he used to blackmail us: "Give me a kiss or I'll sing *Mehbooba, mehbooba* . . ."'

A faint hint of a smile touched Chitra's face and she nodded.

'He went to Jhankar studio and got this song recorded specially for my birthday.'

Manasi placed the cassette in the player. As the music started, Jaidev's baritone filled the whole room. The John Denver number was his favourite one, which he often hummed to himself when he thought no one was listening:

I'll walk in the rain by your side,
I'll cling to the warmth of your hand,
I'll do anything to keep you satisfied,
I love you more than anybody can . . .

Chitra looked at Manasi, fighting back her urge to cry. She saw no tears in Manasi's eyes, only a kind of quiet strength, which she had often seen in Jaidev's eyes.

'Mama, you were right. Papa is dead. But he is not gone, he is here with me in my thoughts, in my memories, in every little thing I do. I'll carry this cassette with me wherever I go. This is Papa's dowry, and will remain with me forever.'

Ramendra Kumar

Forgiveness

The city of Mumbai has seen many riots, but the one that is often referred to as the Bombay Riots, are the ones that took place in response to the demolition of the Babri Masjid in 1992.

On my visit to Bombay (now Mumbai) a couple of years after the backlash against innocent Hindus in 1993 and the subsequent violence against innocent Muslims thereafter, my friend Alyque Padamsee urged me to visit Dharavi, an area that was most affected by the riots.

Our guide took us to a man in his sixties, sitting alone by his home, now partly in ruins. He smiled and shook our hands and talked about the devastation. He led us on to some of the shanties where life had come to a standstill for months after the carnage. Today, after many years, it looked like the ones who survived were ready to move on in life. He pointed at a terrace and said, 'That is where a six-year-old girl was thrown down into a fire.' He gestured to some place else to narrate another gruesome story.

We returned to his home after a brief tour, which left me visibly shaken. Finally he pointed to his own home and told us in the same, even tone as before, how his two sons were butchered in front of him. He was done with tears a long time ago, although the scars were very visible by the sheer absence of feeling. I asked him whether he was still angry. He explained that his grandchildren were very angry, but what was the use? Anger would not bring his sons back to him.

As we parted he said to me, 'Don't ever be angry if something like this happens to you. If I were angry and wanted revenge I would go out and kill the sons of some other parent. And I would make them suffer the way I do now. I do not want anyone to suffer like I do. Not even the murderers of my children.'

I waited till I was in a taxi before I began to cry. I felt privileged that I had encountered a person with such fortitude and wisdom. He had shown me that the only way to end violence in this world is through compassion and forgiveness.

Mahesh Dattani

His Bumper Sticker Reads, 'Princess on Board'

I lost my husband when my daughter was born. She mesmerised him barely a few seconds old. I remember looking up at him after the drama of the birth, wanting reassurance that the baby had all her toes and fingers. And I will never forget the look on his face as he gazed down at her. He created her; she even looks like him. From then on, I was merely the photocopy machine.

After growing up with two sisters, he did think a son would be nice. A son to watch cricket on TV with, to discuss the innards of a car, to share the rock albums of his youth ... all the father-son plans became irrelevant the first time he held his baby daughter. And the minutes-old baby looked up at him, a knowing gleam already in her eyes; she knew this man was wrapped around her little finger—for life.

The little princess is now two years old. She does not like his music, and he now dances to her more melodic (in my opinion) choices. He first condescended to watch, then looked forward to, her incessant demands for Tom and Jerry. Yes, they do share the car—he takes his princess for a spin. When we moved cities, to my frustration he took his time in finalising a house—his choice had to be, as he said, worthy of her! She insists on wearing her Baba's favourite clothes after the day's play is done, so that, 'Baba will say oh my feetopie' when he returns from office. She has figured that, with one little whisper, 'Baba, kaju', her Baba will drop his remote, stop watching TV and get up to oblige her (a feat I have not managed in all the time we have been married).

With me she knows her treats are limited, her TV restricted to certain programmes at certain times of the day, and she better have her milk or else. . . . She also knows that when it is her father's turn to take care of her, she will be taken in royal style to the club swimming pool and not merely to the local park And is sure to get ice-cream instead of a glass of milk. I am the wicked witch in her life!

To him, she is the lode star, the one he comes home to after the stress of work, the one he spends his Sundays with, the one he misses and calls home to find out what she has been up to. I have been relegated to being the ogre in their lives who announces, 'Bed-time'.

I have watched him holding her close, absorbing her baby smells. Treasuring her baby looks, imagining what she will look like all grown-up. Enthralled by the look of peace on a very mobile face as she sleeps. Playing 'here comes the bride' in his head when she bursts from her room demanding his attention to her new pink frock. Watching the man change into a father, anticipating the day when his baby announces, 'Baba, there is someone I want you to meet', and in will walk the scruffiest, the least approvable boyfriend a girl could possibly have!

I guess my own father, in his own way and his own generation and time, felt the same way. Watching my husband with his own little girl, I've learnt to appreciate more the man who made me *his* princess.

Monisha Sen

How Will You Know When It Is for Real?

'How will you *know* when it is for real?' my best friend asked, her voice tinged with frustration.

She was frustrated because I had just fallen in love for the thirty-sixth time.

We were house doctors in our alma mater. She had followed my love lives through four-and-a-half years of medical college, through internship, and she was still there, sympathetic but frustrated, through house job number two.

'I will know,' I said, confident as only a dyed-in-the-wool romantic can be. Had any of the heroines in my beloved Mills and Boons ever *not* known true love when it hit them in the face? I would know.

'You are such a scaredy cat!' Ranj hadn't given up. She was determined to get me to admit that I was a flibberty-gibbet! 'You only moon over unattainable men! Your love affairs are always one-sided! They are not even love affairs; they are just . . .' she shook her head trying to find the right word. 'They are just *crushes*! You are not really looking for commitment.'

I was crushed! To have my thirty-six great loves reduced to the level of crushes was heartbreaking, yet something held me back from making a scathing retort. Instinctively, I knew Ranj was right. She knew me as well as I knew myself. My epic love life was just time-pass. I would moon over a guy because he played great basketball, or taught us amazing surgical concepts. The tell-tale sign was that there were common factors to all my loves, and Ranj had hit the nail on the head; the men invariably had to be shorter than me, and they had to ignore me completely! *Gosh!* I thought. *I don't really want to be in love. I am just in love with the drama of unrequited love!*

I examined the evidence: I never, ever made calf-eyes at men taller than me. I always promptly fell out of love when the object of my affection turned around and gave me a second glance.

I was just not ready to make a commitment, I realised, shocked. I *was* a scaredy-cat! I glared balefully at my best friend for removing the shades from my eyes! My thirty-sixth love affair turned to ashes minutes after it started!

Then my sister, Tin, older by fifteen months, succumbed to the charms of a 'suitable boy' in the Indian Army, and got married. Immediately, I began to feel the pressure of family expectations. The search began. It was a tough call. He would have to be taller than me (I am five-feet ten in my bare feet); a doctor (my wish) and of my faith (my family's wish). And he would have to *not* be from the Defence services (I had them all of my growing years, I did not want any more wheels on my feet!).

This was scary business. I remembered Ranj's words, 'How will you know?'

What if I didn't know? What if I made a ghastly mistake?

The first potential spouse I was scheduled to meet was a doctor born and bred in America. That was easy! I didn't want to settle abroad. He was eye-candy but I felt no tingle.

The next one was eye-candy too; a doctor, tall (obviously!), and nerdy. But there was a flip side. He was thirty-two to my twenty-three years, and a 'feet-firmly-planted-on-the-earth'

Virgo to my 'flighty' Sagittarius. Nevertheless, I tingled and my heart sang; but I was thirty-six times bitten, so I decided not to jump in both feet first. We met again, we chatted medicalese, I still felt the electricity.

So far so good, I thought. *Let's see if I turn tail and run, like I always do.*

And then he said the words that were to change my life for ever.

'There is something you need to know,' he said, looking fearlessly into my eyes. 'I have a hole in the heart, a small one, but nevertheless something you should know about before you make up your mind.'

Whoosh! In the time it took him to catch his breath I had made up my mind. The man was precious. Not only did he make the blood sing in my veins, but he was as intrepid and honest as any Army man. If he was honest about potentially incriminating data *before* I said yes, what talents was I going to discover after we were married?

As far as I was concerned, the deal was clinched. But I wasn't about to make it easy for him. I racked my brains for something that I could use to scare him off.

'Well, er . . .' I said, not to be outdone. 'I have stretch marks on my back. And that's a chickenpox scar on my forehead.'

I waited.

He smiled. 'I guess you grew tall so fast, your cellulite couldn't keep up. And that round mark on your forehead? I can barely see it!'

A handsome hunk with a sense of humour?

'So when do we get married?' I asked, impatient as only a Sagittarian can be.

'Take your time,' the Virgo said. 'Why don't you let your parents decide?'

Would wonders never cease? A *patient* handsome hunk with a family feeling, and a sense of humour! Just what the doctor ordered. Twenty-three happily married years later, as I sit writing this, I realise that you *can* tell when the real thing stares you in the face.

Upreet Dhaliwal

If Mom Had Been Around

My mother succumbed to breast cancer when I was only six years old, but dad, who was still very young then, decided not to marry again. He was a single parent in a cynical Indian society with its notions and prejudices, and his task was not an easy one to accomplish: bringing up a girl.

I am now twenty years old, and the last fourteen years have been most trying, more so, for my father. He did not bring me up like most parents in middle-class south Indian families do, with strong notions of 'good and bad' and 'right and wrong'. I grew up as a tomboy who was always in jeans, sported short hair since I can remember, forever hanging out in some part of the city, never home on time, rebellious to the point of being ridiculous, equally sociable with people of all ages and kinds and doing obscurely random things that no one approved of. Though at times he didn't like certain things I did, he never stopped me from doing them.

This always made me the 'different' child in my extended family. They still loved me, but wished I would be like them, a feat they are still trying to accomplish.

I do not know if it was my position as a child being brought up by a single father or the fact that I was so glaringly different from the others I knew, that made people say things about me. But somehow, I was in the wrong books of many people just for being myself. People who knew my mother always began their sentences with, 'If her mother had been around ...' and went on say how differently I would have been brought up. Though I never paid much heed to it, I slowly began to see the effect it had on my father.

As I grew older, the comments became more frequent and mostly from people he did not expect it from. He took it as a personal insult to his upbringing of his daughter, whom, until then, he had thought he had done a pretty good job with.

I slowly began to realise the trauma he was going through but did not know how to help him. He began to ask me to change my ways in order to please everyone around him. I understood where he stood; he had struggled for a long time, and was now being made to feel like he had made mistakes.

One day, when I could take it no more, I went up to him and asked, 'Pa, why would you want me to change into someone I cannot be? I have done nothing wrong.' He said, 'Maybe they're right. I think I have failed. Maybe you'd have been better off had your mom been there.'

I held his hand and said, 'If mom had been around, we might have never been so close, I might have never spent my childhood being the apple of your eye, I may not have known how great a father you could be, I wouldn't have had the childhood you gave me, I may have never found a shopping partner in you, I may have never run to you when I was afraid of the dark or found you awake the many nights when I was sick, I wouldn't have grown up thinking I am blessed to have you as my dad and answered, "my father", when my teacher asked me whom I admired the most. You may have never introduced me to your amazing knowledge of books and music, I wouldn't have been so possessive about you, I wouldn't have found a confidant for all my girly secrets, I wouldn't have known that no one can keep a secret better than you, I wouldn't have found the man who went to every publishing house in the city to satisfy the whims of a twelve-year-old who thought she could write, nor would I worry everyday if I could ever repay you, but most importantly I would never have found my best friend in you.'

He smiled, said 'Ditto' and walked out of the room.

Those comments still continue to come, but he just smiles and nods them away.

Anusha Parthasarathy

Meeting Kamla

Joe Gallagher was a rotund man. With a white unkempt beard that was braided at the end, a balding head, thick glasses, and a big paunch, Joe could barely see his feet if he looked down.

He inhaled deeply. His pollen allergies notwithstanding, he loved to walk out over the carefully manicured lawns to smell the green grass. It was around ninety degrees in Rolla, Missouri on this bright sunny morning.

His near-deaf ears picked up the shrieks of an emergency vehicle, shattering the peace of that pristine morning. He turned around and saw a giant red-and-white fire truck careen towards one of those identical-looking, brown-and-beige townhouses in Stonebridge.

His otherwise predictable day of watching *M.A.S.H.* reruns and walking around the mall for exercise had just changed tracks.

It was generally considered rude to stare, but he wanted to inquire if everything was fine. Surely, a little neighbourly concern would not be unappreciated.

In the distance, by the fire truck, there was a commotion. Joe could see a fragile, old woman draped in an off-white and red sari. 'Why would someone drape themselves in multiple layers of fabric on this sweltering summer day?' Joe wondered.

A big, red, circular dot graced the centre of her forehead. Her greying hair was braided into a tight knot and her gold earrings caught the sunlight and gleamed. Her middle-aged son was trying to pacify her whilst talking animatedly to the burly firemen at the same time.

Apparently, the fire was the result of a daily religious ritual gone haywire. In the past, Joe had heard ringing bells and her mellifluous voice singing in some language. He had also observed groups of families in bright clothes and ornaments arriving over the weekends to meet, greet, chant and chat.

Today, while trying to light incense sticks for her ritual prayer, the matches had accidentally set some nearby papers on fire. The firemen left after her son had convinced them that this was not a daily occurrence.

Over the following weeks, the old lady often caught Joe's eye on his daily walks. They smiled politely at each other. The smiles eventually changed to words. Joe learnt that her name was Kamala and that her son was a professor at the university. He learnt that the exotic smells from their kitchen were Kamala's own doing. She loved to talk about her cooking and her prayers.

One day, as he walked past, he heard her beautiful voice singing a prayer. He learnt that it was an invocation to a powerful female goddess called Abhirami, to bestow knowledge, wealth, good friends and health upon her son.

Joe was intrigued. He called himself an Irish descendant and as 'proof' of his heritage, he had the mandatory shamrock festoons in his basement kept for St. Patrick's Day celebrations, and he also participated heartily in the festival's famed drinking binges. He suddenly recalled a verse written on the counter of the Irish pub where he had bartended in his younger days.

May love and laughter light your days,
and warm your heart and home.

May good and faithful friends be yours,
wherever you may roam.
May peace and plenty bless your world
with joy that long endures.
May all life's passing seasons
bring the best to you and yours.

That night, Joe found himself wondering about that verse; about his forefathers and what home and friends had meant to them. Joe's wife had died many years ago, and his only daughter was now in New York, leading the busy life of an investment banker. They met each other about once a year.

His thoughts drifted to his friends. A lot of his work buddies had died over the past few years, leaving his Tuesday poker nights a mere roll-call of the survivors. When would it be his turn? How would someone find him? How long would it take? Joe felt uneasy at these thoughts.

As he walked by Kamala's house the next day, he decided to go in. She treated him to some strong Malabar tea and homemade samosas. He observed a long, wooden, stringed instrument in a corner. 'This is called a veena . . .' she said, and proceeded to sit on the floor and play it. She sang a continuation of the verse which she sang daily, about the powerful female goddess. 'It means, "May you have an untiring heart, love, wealth, unfailing words, a just ruler, and a heart that worships Thee".' she explained loudly. By now, she was quite familiar with Joe's hearing problem.

What made the gentle Kamala leave behind her comfortable home in India and come here? Joe wondered. He thought about giving up everything at Rolla and moving to New York to be with his daughter. The city would suffocate him to death. Not that his daughter would be particularly pleased with this idea. Her fast-paced lifestyle did not allow her to have any social life, let alone take in an old man.

Kamala's son entered the room and touched her feet. Her

face contorted into an innocent smile. As if reading Joe's thoughts, she remarked, 'He is very caring and thoughtful. It was difficult, at first, living in a strange country. But gradually I made friends. I have my prayers, cooking and the veena. Most importantly, I have my son. I hope he gets married soon. I am looking forward to the day when I can pamper my grandkids and teach them to play the veena . . .' her face lit up like the moon.

Maybe the Irish were right, Joe pondered that night. Maybe everyone needed to believe in something bigger than themselves—to write verses, to bless people, and to pass on goodwill to future generations. Were his Gaelic forefathers watching him right now? What did his own name mean?

He spent the rest of the night in front of his computer. Browsing through a database of Irish names and coats of arms and other historical information, he finally found that 'Gallagher' meant 'someone who liked foreigners'. He smiled.

It was around six in the morning. Bright red lights whizzed past his bedroom. Joe got dressed and stepped out. He could see the fragile, exhausted frame of Kamala in a stretcher.

Two days later, he saw the same group of families, dressed in pristine white. A sea of slippers were kept outside Kamala's door. A shaven-headed, bare-chested professor stood outside the house, ready to perform his mother's last rites. 'My mother was fond of you. She wanted you to have this,' he said, as Joe walked by the house hesitantly.

Joe was at a loss for words. It was a piece of monogrammed paper, with Kamala's own calligraphy on it. It was the last verse of her daily prayer.

'My mother used these words to tell me the story of how the Hindu deity Abhirami was Lord Shiva's wife as well as Lord Vishnu's sister. I guess this is her way of saying that we are all related, either by blood, or by love. . . .' her son said softly. And he turned and walked inside.

Joe stood outside the patio for a minute. Slowly, he walked towards the door and paused. He then bent down to take off his shoes before walking into the living-room, full of people.

Sangeetha Parthasarthy

Not So Ordinary

My home is in Rambaug colony in Pune. There are eighteen bungalows in a row in the colony. Ours is the seventh one. There was one speciality in our colony: in each bungalow there was one pet dog. We too had one, but we didn't have any fancy breed: we had an Indian pye-dog. My mother had found him at our farm in Daund, one hour from Pune. It was only five months old at the time. We called him Moti.

My mother loved the dog very much, but for some reason I wasn't too fond of him. I always wanted a special dog like an Alsatian, Doberman, Pug or Samoyed as my pet, but I knew my mother would refuse to get me another pet when we already had one. I would always say, 'Mom what's special in a simple dog, let's get a dog like our neighbours,' and she would always reply, 'A dog is a dog; it doesn't matter if it's simple or special.'

Though Moti was a pye-dog, he looked stronger than an Alsatian because of my mother's proper nourishment. My mother would always first feed Moti and then have her meal. Every morning, my mother would give Moti milk and dog biscuits. If there was less milk at home, she would borrow some from a neighbour, but would never leave Moti hungry. Moti was so attached to my mother, that he would only eat food that my mother gave him by her hand. That is why my mother always avoided going out of station for more than a day. Moti would just stay hungry if the food was not given by my mother's hand.

One day, most of the people in the society were away, attending the wedding ceremony of a neighbour. The ceremony was at a hall just twenty minutes away from our society. The wedding finished in the evening; my mother was in hurry to return as she had to feed Moti. When we entered the colony, we saw cops everywhere. We asked the cops what was the matter, and we found out that several houses, with locks on the outside, had been robbed. Ours was locked from outside too, but we hadn't been robbed.

Police investigation later revealed that it was a planned robbery. The thieves had fed the dogs in our colony with biscuits that had drugs which rendered them unconscious. Moti had not eaten those biscuits, as it was not given to him by my mother. With tears in her eyes, my mother said me, 'Now I know that ordinary dogs are not ordinary—they are even more special than others.' And I agreed.

Nikhil Kulkarni

Overcoming an Addiction

Many times in life, we come across individuals who, with the sheer strength of their willpower and determination, have fought and emerged victorious against a bad habit or a vice. I feel proud to be related to one such fighter: my father.

We are a family of four—my father (a retired school principal), my mother (a homemaker), my elder sister (a school principal) and I. My sister is married (my brother-in-law is a government employee), stays in the same city and has a thirteen-year-old daughter.

My father, currently sixty-five years old, had been addicted to chewing tobacco for around twenty-five years. We had tried all possible ways to make him kick this bad habit, but unfortunately, all our efforts were in vain. He would give up chewing tobacco for four–five days and then return to it, citing stress as an excuse. Making him read press clippings, articles, or watch media promos on the hazardous effects of tobacco could not make him see reason either. His constant counter-argument was, 'My food habits are very good. I eat all those vegetables/fruits which contain anti-carcinogenic nutrients.' My mother, religious soul that she is, had left everything to her God, hoping that he would weave a miracle that would make my father give up his addiction! And for all you non-believers reading this, the miracle did take place!

This happened seven years back, when my niece was around six years old. She had come down to stay with us during her summer vacations and was one day sitting with my father at the study table, each engrossed in their work. As was his habit, my father would occasionally take out a packet of tobacco and put a handful in his mouth. My niece asked him curiously, 'What are you chewing? Please give me some of it.' My mother, who was also sitting in the same room, was as shocked as my father and they didn't know how to react. My niece continued in the same vein and then Papa said, to humour her, 'I cannot give you what I am having as it is bad for your health.' She turned back with the arrogance that only a grandchild can have and said, 'If it is bad, then why are you having it Dada?'

It was then that the actual enormity of his vice sunk in and my father immediately threw away the tobacco packet. Since then, he has never gone back to his addiction.

For me, there were three learning lessons in this experience: It is never too late to give up a bad habit—my father was fifty-eight years old when he kicked his. Love for someone can weave a miracle—it was my father's love for his granddaughter and his mental strength that made him give up a vice he'd had for more than two decades. And sheer willpower and determination are enough to see you through.

Huta Raval

Power

To know that I can say a few words,
And by saying them, I can destroy you,
Not because those words were said,
But because I said them to you.

That is the power I hold over you.

Then to realise that I never will say them,
My heart which hurts if another harms you,
Would break if it knew that I be the cause,
Of a single tear of pain in your eyes.

That is the power you hold over me.
Your whip, you've handed to me willingly,
Mine you do hold with my consent,
Both of us know that neither will use it.

And we go on as a willing slave to the other.

That is power we hold over each other.

Malavika Thiagaraja

The Art of Admonition

Once upon a time, when I was young, grown-ups had a special way of addressing us youngsters. They would assume a slightly annoyed air, frown, and, more often than not, shake a forefinger at you. Then, in a special hoarse voice, they would get whatever they had to off their chest. It's not as if they had anything more forbidding to say than what youngsters today have to endure, it's just the way they said it that unsettled me.

Mind you, not all grown-ups spoke in that manner. At school, for instance, there was Father Beech who, in his chattiest tone, would invite you up to his room, to explain why the homework he had set was best not left undone. There, his manner continued to be as pleasant as before, while he left it to a springy, malacca cane to do the explaining for him, as he applied it zestfully to the seat of your pants. Needless to say, homework—well, Fr. Beech's homework, anyway—could not have achieved higher priority in a schoolboy's crowded schedule.

I often asked myself whether I preferred Fr. Beech's endearing manner, with his twinkling eyes and mischievous smile, along with the ever-present risk of being caned or, by contrast, the more prevalent mode of admonition, namely the special hoarse voice and all that went with it. The latter was exemplified by one of my aunts who, I hasten to add, was really a kindly soul who meant no harm. I reached different conclusions at different times. Straight after an encounter with Fr. Beech, and still smarting fiercely from the application of his cane, I'd vow that nothing could be so unacceptable; the padre's cheerful demeanour et cetera, notwithstanding. At other times, thoroughly put off by my aunt's exaggerated expostulations at something as ordinary and inevitable as my dishevelled appearance after climbing a tree, I would smart every bit as much at being talked down to by an adult. After swinging back and forth, from the informality of Fr. Beech on the one hand, to the needlessly stern attitude of my aunt on the other, my conclusion was that Fr. Beech's method of communication was preferable by far, provided he forsook the use of his cane. How effective his pleasantly delivered words would be, without the backing of his preferred instrument of torture, was another matter entirely.

On my attaining adulthood, when I could no longer be targeted by the likes of Fr. Beech or my aunt, the urge to reflect upon and judge their respective modes of putting across their point of view, ceased to concern me ... until I found myself the father of a rebellious pre-teenage daughter.

'Disgraceful!' I declared one day, after reading her school report which was riddled with remarks like, 'Could do better if she tried' and 'Persists in reading comics in class, despite repeated warnings'.

I brought myself to look suitably outraged.

'What do you mean by reading comics in class?' I demanded, glaring at her.

'Those must be the ones I borrowed from Mary Fernandes. She wanted them back before the end of the period,' explained my daughter in an off-handed manner.

'You dare come up with your ridiculous excuses,' I retorted, and took a swipe at her posterior with the flat of my hand.

'Hey, cut out the rough stuff,' protested the lass, skipping nimbly out of range, and striking a heroic but baffling pose.

'What's that supposed to be?' I enquired, pointing to her stance. 'Bharatnatyam?'

'No, karate ... that's what!' she replied defiantly.

Try as I might, I could not help myself, and burst out laughing. 'You mean you'd use karate on your poor old moth-eaten Daddy?' I said, and gathering her up in my arms, I kissed her.

'You should hear the way you spoke to me,' she complained, 'like old Mr Bogeyman himself!'

'How should I have spoken?'

'Like my Daddy speaking to a young lady, that's how!'

'Okay,' I said. 'No speaking like old Mr Bogeyman on my part and, on yours, no reading comics in class; or anything else you are accused of in that dreadful report. How's that?'

'Okay,' she replied with a noncommittal air, 'we'll give it a try.'

Since then, through the years, we still have our moments of heated confrontation, and though it now occurs purely on the verbal level, I am reminded that words too can hurt. My daughter gives me one of her special warning looks over the top of her steel-rimmed spectacles, which tells me that what I have to say needs to be said better; and if that fails to elicit the right response, the young lady simply slips into the karate posture I once mistook for bharatnatyam. The message then comes through with startling clarity, and I correct myself at once.

Pesi Padshah

The Captain and I

It is one of those long-drawn, balmy Mumbai nights that assures you that you are alone in that absolute, acid-dripping sense of the word. Alone at the mercy of self.

My eyes hurt. I have enough of the cheap Irving Wallace and my wife's snoring. I part the curtains and look down from the window. The view of the shadowy street thirty floors below is dark, distorted, dangerous; almost inviting.

No matter what my wife says, I don't have a TV in my place and that's a big plus for a man like me. I switch on the drawing room lights, and hear the clear gongs of two from the nearby church tower. No signs of elusive, comforting shroud of sleep for me.

I think of an easy way, a Campos; but that would make it the eighteenth this month. No. I walk into the kitchen and think food. Maybe a grilled potato-and-pea sandwich and a hot cuppa, but I remember the doctor's preaching about caffeine and cholesterol. I suppress my urge.

The scratched sticker of Mickey Mouse on the fridge brings back distant memories, and I feel a pull that takes me to the old table in my study.

Unlike most people, I have placed my table against a blank wall. Captain stands alone on that table. He is a four-and-a-half-inch plastic soldier clad in military fatigues and laced boots. My son used to wear the green beret of the same style, pulled at the same rakish angle, when he was five. That boy could talk and play with Captain for hours.

It is my turn to talk with Captain tonight.

'Hullo Captain,' I say and flop down in the chair.

Captain looks at me and says nothing.

'It's 2 a.m. and my wife is fast asleep, everything is silent and understood,' I say. There is something touching about the way Captain smiles.

I offer my hand to Captain and look into his eyes till I feel the bitter sting of my tears.

'Call him,' Captain says. 'It's a cool morning out there.'

So I call my son who lives eight thousand miles from here, somewhere in a Seattle suburb. I catch him on his way to work, and hear the traffic before his voice.

He takes his time to respond, and that's a good thing for me. I am not good at talking weather and things, but I try for a few minutes till he cuts me short.

'Dad, it must be three in the morning there.'

It is Dad, always; he never calls me father. He is more American than most Americans.

'Wait,' I say. 'Your mother wants to talk to you.' I wake up my wife in a hurry.

'Rohan is on the line.' I hand the phone over to her.

After a few groggy words of greeting, her motor mouth gets going. In that half hour, she smiles, cries, threatens, argues, warns, and pleads. She updates him about the latest crop of girls in her circle of influence. What is right and what is proper according to the holy *Gita*, and the latest price of carrots at the street corner.

'Lemon pickle,' she announces at the top of her voice, 'is the best medicine for indigestion.'

I do a series of palm-and-fingers gestures in her face, and convey the pulse rate per second.

'He is driving, save the juicy stuff for later,' I say loudly enough so that my son can get the message.

She finally hears the click at the other end and turns to me. 'You called him. He would never call at this hour.'

'Your tech-nut is still with the same woman?' I ask.

'Are you taking an off tomorrow? Just look at the watch.' She straightens her pillow and goes back to snoring in two-and-a-half seconds.

I switch off the light and walk out of the stuffy bedroom.

On the table, Captain is back to having the same cryptic expression on his tiny face. If I talk to him the next time, he would say something like, 'I almost saved your life that night.'

Mahendra Waghela

The Cheesy Romance That Wasn't

We had gone to university together, then drifted apart as mere acquaintances often do. A decade later, we found each other on Facebook, and spent a few days discovering what the other had become. I really don't know what he made of the person I am, but to me, he was one half of a perfect couple—two good-looking, much-in-love people, each doing very well professionally. The photographs he posted on Facebook were almost idyllic—a tall, dark, even if not quite handsome man and his pretty, chirpy, well-dressed wife enjoying each other's company in the most idyllic holiday spots.

They brought in the New Year in Bali. Holidayed in Italy a few weeks later. Summer was spent in the chill of an Australian winter. Hong Kong was where they celebrated five years of married life. In-between were birthdays, movie premiers, excursions. There were photographs of her, there were photographs of him, and there were photographs of them—hugging, eating, drinking, always smiling. They were, in one word, perfect.

'Tina and I spent the weekend working out "what if" scenarios,' he wrote as his status message a few months back, 'and in the best scenario, we still got together. Pretty good going that.' All my life, I have been addicted to constructing 'what if' scenarios, but every time I indulged myself, I emerged as someone quite different from what I was. I may have been perfectly happy with my existence, but when I played 'what if', I always wanted something to be different. Oh that anyone can be so satisfied with life as to not want to be anywhere else! It was cute; it was also a teeny bit cheesy.

Occasionally, when a new photo album was uploaded, or a status update posted, I wondered about their relationship. Were they really as perfect a couple as he projected? On the other extreme, could that golden couple bit just be a façade that hid a marriage that existed in name only? I never knew the person well enough to ask, and nor could I ask mutual friends the same blatantly; after all, what concern of mine was someone else's romance?

'Tina has left me and gone to live with God', he wrote on Facebook on Monday. I read it, but the implication didn't register till an hour later. It was not a sudden whim that had carted his wife off to the feet of a guru; she had really and truly left the world. There are hundreds of messages of condolence on his Facebook page, while his wife continues to grin impishly from her profile picture.

But one half of the golden couple is missing.

I left my condolences with the rest of the wreathes on his Facebook page. But really all I wanted to do was scream 'why?' and 'how'? But of course, one is always too polite to ask such questions.

It was through a mutual friend of the couple that I found out that she had been diagnosed with cancer just before their marriage. She started undergoing chemotherapy soon after their wedding, but the cancer never went into remission. Every single day of their marriage, they knew that she did not have too long to live. They knew they had, at best, a couple of years to live their life, and they lived it as best as they could. They tried to live as full a life as they could.

'Counting the minutes till Tina lands back in Bangkok', he'd written about a month back. 'Too many minutes!' At that time, it seemed almost impossibly romantic that someone could think like that after five years of marriage—had I encountered the line in a book, I would definitely have sniggered. Now I know it was just the anguish of a man who knows he has only a few more moments together, at having some of those precious moments being snatched away.

Cheesy it may have seemed, but true love it definitely was.

Rayna Talwar

The Cheque

It was a balmy monsoon evening in June. I was sitting alone in our favourite café in Bandra, Mumbai. Anil had just left the café, and I needed some time to myself before heading back home.

He had left with a promise that we'd meet for dinner the next night to bring in my birthday. We'd met after a week, and for the millionth time, my 'I love you Anil' was met with just a gentle squeeze of my hand and a smile.

I had met him at the workplace eight months ago. He was the love of my life. He knew that. And I knew he was crazy about me too. Then *why* couldn't he just say it?

'Am I being too hasty? Doesn't he want to commit? I can't take this anymore!' I wailed into the phone as my cousin Neha pretended to listen. Neha was eighteen, loved playing tennis and only spoke to guys who were interested in trying to beat her on the courts.

'It's my birthday tomorrow! There's nothing I want more than for Anil to say "I love you" to me. Do you think he's been waiting for that? For my birthday?'

'Errr ... I dunno,' was all I could get out of her. She seemed distracted, as usual.

'Never mind. I'll see you tomorrow Negs,' I sighed.

The next evening, I waited for Neha to pick me up. I didn't

want to mention anything about Anil to my parents yet, so my excuse to them was that we were having dinner with some friends for my birthday. Neha came promptly at 8.30 p.m., dropped me off at the Taj Land's End Hotel, and said she'd be back to fetch me, 'at sharp 12.15 a.m.'

'Thanks Negs ... I owe you one,' I said gratefully as I stepped out of the car.

'No sweat! Tell Anil I said hi,' she said in her usual bored tone, and zipped off.

I entered the lobby and there he was, wearing a smart black (new?) shirt, clean-shaven, smelling nice and beaming at the sight of me.

'Yippee ... I'm spending my birthday with you!' I said as he hugged me tight.

'I know! I was worried Neha was going to call and say you can't make it. Anyway, we're here and we can have a nice long dinner,' he said as we quickly went up to the restaurant and settled into a corner table. The waitress who escorted us was smiling widely.

Anil looked a bit fidgety, I noticed.

He insisted on drinks first. Mocktails, since we were both teetotallers. 'Sure Anil, although I prefer soup ...'

'Oh after some time ... we have plenty of time, don't we?'

After forty-five minutes of sipping a mocktail, I was hungry enough to eat *him*. He finally agreed to order appetisers.

'I love you Anil,' I ended up telling him yet again. *I'm pushing my luck. What if he gets up and walks away one of these days* ... were the kind of thoughts running around in my head as soon as I said it.

But he didn't get up. He just gave me that smile again.

Aargh! I'm going to die old and alone, was how my brain reacted to that smile.

But my mood quickly changed back. It was a treat for us to get that much time to ourselves and we soon relaxed, joked and talked endlessly. The food was great, and the evening was turning out to be a lovely one. Not to mention that the restaurant staff kept giving me these dazzling smiles.

Ah! I'm getting a cake at midnight I think. That's his big surprise ... I was sure of it.

Soon enough, it was midnight. Anil got up, came round and gave me a big hug. The smiling waitress brought in an enormous bouquet of red roses, followed by the smiling manager, cake in tow. Neha popped in a few minutes later with a couple of friends and it turned out to be quite the predictable celebration that I'd expected. I gave up all my aspirations for Anil's 'I love you Sheetal'.

We soon left the restaurant, and Neha offered to drop Anil to the station. My spirits dipped as we all bundled ourselves into the car in the blinding rain.

Just as we got out of the hotel gate, Anil leaned towards Neha and said, 'Ahem ... Neha, you think you could drop us out here for a bit?'

'What? Anil ...' I started.

'Eh? Sure,' said Neha at the same time.

'Thanks Neha ... could you guys drive around for fifteen minutes or so?' Anil asked her, without even a glance at my perplexed face.

'Sure. No problem,' she said, without batting an eyelid. Neha was like that. Never surprised by anything.

And with that, Anil took my hand and whisked me out into the rain. Neha drove off, and we walked onto the promenade lacing the seafront and stood there. It was quite a romantic setting, now that I think of it. But at the time, I was thoroughly confused. This was a really romantic Anil, and a romantic Anil is not someone I knew!

'I haven't given you a birthday gift,' he said softly, holding me closer.

'Hmm, but I know you. You probably went to ten places

and didn't know what to get! I wasn't expecting anything,' I said, somewhat shyly.

He smiled again. 'I do have a gift for you. It's right here in my shirt pocket. Here, take it yourself.'

I reached into his pocket, hands trembling, and drew out an envelope. I opened it, and found ... a folded cheque.

'Umm ... I hope you're not going to pay me for the dinner,' I said, laughing lamely.

'No, Sheetal. Open it,' he said, suddenly all serious.

It was a regular bank cheque. And yet, I couldn't believe what I was seeing. In his scrawny handwriting, Anil had drawn it out to 'MRS SHEETAL ANIL GOEL'.

'Anil ... Wha ... WHAT?' I couldn't believe it. He was proposing?!

When I finally looked up, I saw that he had tears in his eyes, just like I did. 'Sheetal, will you marry me? Not today, not tomorrow ... whenever you're ready. See ...' he said pointing to the cheque in my trembling hands, '... I haven't put a date on it. Whenever you wish, you can fill that in and let me know.'

'Anil ... really?' I thought I was dreaming.

'Yes really. And one more thing ...' he said, moving a stray lock of hair away from my face, 'I love you sweetheart. Very much. I'm sorry I haven't told you this before. I just don't believe in love without commitment, and I wasn't ready to commit until I was capable of it. I'm sorry ... so sorry I haven't said this before ... I love you very, very much ...'

I remember those words clearly, but my recollection of that night is still hazy, since I was seeing Anil through a curtain of tears through it all. I vaguely remember Neha zipping back to fetch us, dropping a beaming Anil off to the station after that and then dropping me off home too. ...

I returned the cheque to Anil with a date on it a couple of years later, and we had a wonderful wedding in Mumbai the following year. Neha was my bridesmaid, of course!

It's been another four years since then, and we've just finished redecorating our beautiful little home. And if you ever come by, you will find, amongst the wedding pictures, the cheque framed and holding a place of pride on my family picture wall.

Sheetal Goel

The Divinity of Unconditional Love

Like a seashore in high tide,
My memory has failed
To wash off
The bond between us
because even today,
Hidden in the vast terrain,
there remains a speck,
A grain of sand
even if only a latent desire,
A speck, that is—You ...

There it will remain
for evermore,
until my body
turns to dust,
And that little speck
Returns to its Origins.

It will bring to my mind
Laughter and glee
and when I am desolate,
Company.
It will teach me
what and where
I am wrong
and sometimes,
It will soothe me
with its Silence.

I am its eternal devotee
No one can isolate me
from that tiny speck.

If not your company,
I won't let this go.
If not your touch,
I won't let this fade.
If not your smile,
I won't let this die.

If not you,
This is mine ...

Shriyaa Trivedi

The Poker Room

The white envelope glides towards me again. It's Danish. Danish Khan is a twenty-one-year-old software engineer from Pakistan. He's also my online poker buddy. I am a forty-four-year-old Indian housewife with two grown-up children and a lot of free time on my hands. Bored? Yes, yes I was a bored housewife. Playing poker online helped me, if for a few hours a day, leave behind my staid existence and be a part of something other than household chores and duties.

Our 'poker room' is a small melting-pot, with players from various corners of the globe. There was another lovely girl, Manuella, who joined us all the way from France. Besides bonding over poker, there was also a lot of incessant chatter, good-natured banter and friendly ribbing amidst all of us.

Over a few months, I watched the friendship between Danish and Manuella blossom into something more. Sometimes, I would also be a part of their conversations and play 'agony aunt' to either of them. I could sense that Danish had begun trusting me. One day he was unusually quiet while we played. I wondered if something had happened between Manuella and him. He had also been absent from the poker room for quite a long while ...

After a few days, I decided to chat with him. Our friendship had graduated from being just poker buddies in an online forum. I wanted to ask him a hundred questions but better judgement prevailed. He was very monosyllabic and my heart went out to him. Finally, he typed out, 'Do you believe that you can really fall in love on the net?' I sensed his anguish, but before I could voice my opinion he went on.

'Mano (Manuella) is a doctor in Nice. She's twenty-nine years old and we are both madly in love with each other. We cannot live without each other even for a second.' I let him pour his heart out to me, sensing his need to get all this off his chest. 'I was in love with a girl in college once, but was too shy to tell her. I fantasised about marrying her and believed all my dreams would come true, till one day she left without so much as a good-bye. After a year of searching for her, I finally got her phone number and called her. She couldn't even place me, and when she finally remembered, she just said that I should move on as she had. I was shell-shocked! I could not breathe, as I felt the life-force had been sucked out of me. For months my friends took me to parties, got me to meet other girls, but I never felt the same. It was only after I met Mano that I started feeling alive again. I just know she's my soulmate.'

I took all this in. The poor boy! He had obviously been through a lot, but the good news was that he had met someone else. And yet, he sounded troubled. Could the problem be that a French girl might not be able to adjust in a country like Pakistan? Or was it the age difference? Maybe their parents would never approve. . . .

We started talking about the practicality or rather, the impracticality of the situation, like the fact that he had never travelled outside Pakistan and that it was difficult to get a visa. My pragmatic self surfaced and I tried to reason with him. Their love story spelled disaster; I could only see dark clouds, I said. There was a lump in my throat and I could sense that he was on the verge of tears, but I controlled my emotions and decided it was better to show him harsh reality.

But he seemed very calm and collected when he replied, 'I love Mano, and I will cross every hurdle there is to get her. I breathe only for her, she will be my wife and I will prove you wrong.'

His conviction hit me like a ton of bricks. I could feel my cynicism melting away. Love really can make people climb the highest mountains!

I want to tell Danish that I pray for him every day. I pray that he does get to be with his loved one. He has reaffirmed my faith in love.

I want him to know, that watching his relationship with Manuella evolve, has had a cathartic effect on me. Danish's trials and tribulations made me more appreciative of my life and realise how fortunate I am to have found my soulmate!

Sometimes, we take love for granted and never think twice about hurting our loved ones. We burden them with expectations and sacrifice love at the altar of the material world, never once thinking how good we have it. Sometimes, all it takes is someone else's love story to make us realise that we are lucky to be in one of our own.

Shashi Agarwal

The Wisdom Tooth

'I'm hungry, should we go to the station for egg-bhurji?' she said into the phone excitedly. It was 2 a.m. I smiled. This is what made my friendship with Ritika so precious—we were always doing mad, impulsive things. 'Yes sure,' I said drowsily, 'pick me up in ten minutes.'

As I got dressed, I couldn't stop reflecting on how our friendship had evolved. I had moved to Delhi two years back for work. I was single and eager to make friends. Ritika was ten years older than me, but a child at heart. She helped me settle in like I was family—gas connections, curtains, second-hand furniture, maid, electrician, the works. We spent a lot of time together and grew very close quickly. We'd take walks, cook together, go shopping, whine about work, discuss our relationships, share our dreams—we had become like sisters and I was delighted and grateful to have a close friend in a new city.

It did have its ups and downs though. Six months back, when I started dating Neel, I was often torn between whom to give time to. Ritika too, suddenly realised that I wasn't available as I used to be and had her emotional moments. But there was one time when I almost lost her ...

Ritika had problem teeth and needed to get them checked regularly. One such trip to the dentist revealed that a wisdom tooth had to be extracted, but it was complicated. The root of the neighbouring tooth was slightly entwined with this one and so she would have to deal with some extra pain and bleeding. 'Oh well,' she said jokingly, 'if my wisdom has to go, I'm not going to cling to it.'

The night after the extraction, Ritika was in a lot of pain. She called me, in obvious agony, and asked if I could come over. I was silent. Neel had made time after a long while to go for a movie and I didn't want to cancel our date. 'Sorry baby, I won't be able to make it. Will definitely drop in tomorrow though,' I said. I hung up, and from that moment on there was an uneasy feeling in my belly.

When I called Ritika the next morning, she didn't take my call. More calls followed—with no response. Finally she messaged, 'Need some time alone'. I knew she was angry and hurt and I didn't blame her. I'd been callous and insensitive and was feeling miserable for being so selfish.

Another day passed and by now I was feeling awful and was filled with remorse. Finally, towards the evening, I sent her a message, 'Hey Ritz, want to meet up for a walk?' I waited, hoping she was feeling better. Half an hour later she replied, 'Okay, same place, 6 p.m.'

I went there early. It was one of the most scenic parts in that area—with old trees, loads of butterflies and birds, and we had had many a walk interspersed with long chats here. I paced impatiently till I saw her petite frame arrive in the distance. As she came closer, I could see her face was drawn, from the pain and the drugs that had been prescribed. She looked paler and thinner than when I'd last seen her. I cringed again at my thoughtlessness.

We fell into step and walked in silence for awhile. 'How're you feeling now?' I finally asked meekly. 'Hmm fine, it's still painful though,' she said slowly. We walked some more—quietly, slowly, listening to the birds returning to their homes.

I felt heavy and uneasy, and finally started crying. 'Hey! What's wrong?' Ritika asked concernedly. 'Everything okay with you and Neel?' 'Yes, Ritz,' I said, now sobbing full-throttle, running nose and all. 'I just feel awful about not being there for you . . . I'm so sorry.' I reached out to her and hugged her tight. She gently stroked my head. I knew from that tender touch that my best friend, with her big, beautiful heart had forgiven me and I swore to be more sensitive the next time.

My phone beeped and I emerged out of my reverie. Ritika was downstairs, waiting in her car. I skipped two steps and hurried down. There she was—looking fresh and lively in the middle of the night. With an innocent-looking face that broke into a smile easily. I jumped in, we hugged. 'You won't believe what happened this evening!' she exclaimed. 'What what. Tell me everything!' That was our standard response. 'You know I was stepping out of work when this lady . . .'

Our journey to the station and through life continued. . . .

Puja Madan

United

Rani stared at the clump of hair that had just fallen in front of her. She stared at it in disbelief, and then started screaming, 'Ajay, come here fast!' Her husband came running in from the next room, TV remote control in his hand. He saw the hair and, without a word, held Rani close to him. She was sobbing by this time, Ajay's hands rubbing her shaking back. After a few minutes, they noticed their son, Arun, standing in the doorway. The three-year-old was crying, without even knowing what was wrong. Rani quickly wiped her tears away and ran over to hug him.

This incident was the first of many as Rani continued to lose her hair. The chemotherapy had started recently, so it was expected, but who said that the expected is always welcome? As each clump of hair fell out, Rani became more despondent. She threw away her hair ornaments and stopped using the mirror. One day, when she did look at her reflection, she was horrified and broke the mirror. She stopped going out except for her chemo sessions. Even then, she didn't even look at the doctor, just mechanically went through the ritual. When friends invited them over for dinner, Ajay would say no on their behalf. 'I can't show the world how ugly I am,' said Rani.

One day at the office, Ajay came up with what he thought

was a brilliant idea. He would buy Rani a wig! He went home early and coerced Rani into the car. She looked at him with curiosity because she hadn't seen him this excited in months. In the wig shop, Rani looked at several wigs, trying on each one for Ajay. She classified most of them as 'ugly' until she found the one she liked. It was a wig of shoulder-length hair, silky, black and wavy, just like her own. 'I'll take this,' she told the shopkeeper and walked out smiling, Arun tagging along happily as well.

Rani wore the wig. She wore it to her parents' house. She wore it to her best friend's house. One day, when a friend was visiting their house, the friend's five-year-old said, 'Aunty had no hair last week. How can she have so much hair now?' Rani struggled to find an answer. The child was right, this wasn't her hair. Who was she fooling? Devastated, Rani threw the wig into the trash can and stayed in her room all day until Ajay came home. Arun told him the story and asked, 'Papa, how can we make mama stop crying?'

Ajay had another great idea. 'Come with me, Arun. I have an idea.' The two drove to a hair salon nearby.

At nine o' clock, Rani came out of her room to see if Arun and Ajay had eaten. She found two bald heads beaming at her from in front of the television set. 'Look mama! We're a family of baldies!' he chuckled.

Sudesna Ghosh

Writing for Chicken Soup

There we were, Anil and I, discussing what we could write as a story for the *Chicken Soup for the Indian Romantic Soul*. I had sent in one story already, but it had not yet been selected and I wanted to send in another one. I had experienced moments of love in very unexpected moments, as Anil is extremely selfless and caring. I wanted to write about how love is not just a romanticised term as depicted in movies and novels, but could be felt in unromantic moments too, really nothing-out-of-the-ordinary, domestic moments!

I was telling Anil about my ideas and the miniscule incidents that had driven me to being pretty emotional and appreciative about our relationship. I don't know why, but I then asked him, 'Anil, if you had to write a story about me, what would you write about? Have there been any such moments for you?' He couldn't think of anything! That made me feel a bit rotten, but I could understand, because not only are these moments rare, but we do tend to forget them as quickly as they happen. I couldn't really blame him. I was just about to start writing my story, when he said, 'Actually, I cannot recollect a particular incident right now, but when Bhaiji (his father) passed away, I remember that you were my greatest support system. I could feel your love and that gave me a new reason to live. In the worst time of my life, you were there.'

I could not believe my ears. I was teary-eyed and moved. To say I was happy would be an understatement, because Anil is hardly ever liberal with appreciation! As I hugged him, something occurred to me. 'Anil, during the worst period of my life (when I suffered from rheumatoid arthritis for over one-and-a-half years) you were there for me; during your trials I was there for you, what more could one want in life?'

That was that. My story faded away into the background. The millions of little incidents of 'I am right, you are wrong', 'I wanted this, you did not do it', etc. faded into oblivion, and the only important thing, our love for each other, stood out like the blinking lights at the movies and casinos. Wow. Can you imagine that. Finding love in an unromantic moment. Out of the blue. Thank you, Chicken Soup, for though love is always hanging around somewhere in the background, you pulled it by its collar, and got it out in the forefront for me! For though we know that we love and are loved, these incidents make it fresh and young again! Love is indeed an awesome feeling!

Seema Agarwal

2
OVERCOMING OBSTACLES

We could never learn to be brave and patient if there were only joy in the world.

–Helen Keller

A Different Plane

We were waiting for all eight of us to assemble for practice when the youngest two of the dancers called in sick. The rest of us looked at each other in dismay as the programme was just a week away, and we had learnt this item just two days back. But, well, we assured ourselves, there was at least a week. So we had hope.

As we finished the rehearsal for the day and were chatting, the topic of the girls being unwell came up again. We wondered if they would be able to participate in the programme, and someone suddenly said, 'Oh come! You have done it. I am sure they can too!'

I looked at the person who said this and we smiled with the shared memory.

Yes, I had done the amazing thing, and now—in retrospect—I wonder how!

August 2007. My dance class was conducting its twenty-fifth anniversary programme. I had begged off, as coordinating group practice was becoming a nightmare: I had children to look after, and I might not have been able to rope in my mother to care for them at the specified time. But, as fate would have it, two of the dancers who were part of the show developed trouble with their knees and had to drop out. Finally, one of the women coordinating the show requested me to step in as, for one specific item, they needed a senior dancer and they had exhausted all options.

I agreed, thinking it was but one item. Little did I know what I was letting myself in for. It was extremely complicated and needed group sessions so that we could all put our knowledge together to make sense of this piece on Shiva. We started practice, and as the timings were erratic, I finally surrendered my children to my mother.

Two weeks before the programme, at the end of July, I developed fever and shivering. I rarely fall sick, and fever—once in a blue moon! I tried to will it away, took a Crocin to keep me going. But, to my utter horror, I realised that I was taking a tablet every once in three hours! And every time the fever returned, touching 104 degrees. Shivering accompanied it. I had to give in and find a doctor. I went to a highly recommended GP nearby. She prescribed several tests for me, and even got a malarial test done in her own clinic. All negative. Oh, the usual viral—both of us smiled at each other.

Virals last for three days, right? I could wait it out. Meanwhile, I continued practice, taking Crocin.

Ten days later, the fever showed no signs of abating. I couldn't back out of the programme because, for one, of course, I expected to recover, but also because no one else could have fitted into the group at this stage.

On the programme day, I had to trust Dolo 65 to see me through. I took one before sitting down for make-up. I wore the costume and started my warming up exercises—something I am sometimes not diligent about, but that day, it was critical that I be in form. The programme started—my performance would come later. I watched everybody go on stage and perform with aplomb, their practice showing in the flow of movements. I stood still, wondering if I was going to stand out like sore thumb. In bharatnatyam, half-sitting is very important, and even on a good day, it can defeat dancers. Today, I was sure I would be unable to maintain it and would probably stand through the item as others executed the arai-mandi perfectly.

I went on stage as we took positions in the dark. The raga was played and the lights came on slowly. I flowed with the music. As my guru said the jathi, the legs moved in rhythm with the rest. Suddenly, I was expressing my surrender to Lord Shiva, and indeed, I felt totally one with Him, seeking His guidance to carry me through this. I was one with the music, one with the other dancers, and as a team, we delivered. Where was the pain, the fear, the insecurity? I had forgotten it all as I let the music wash over me and my body respond.

The pain came later, but so did appreciation for not letting a physical limitation take over my dance. Those who didn't know I had danced under these circumstances were surprised and said that they wouldn't have guessed it if I hadn't mentioned it.

My son fell sick as I recovered. He had typhoid. Just as he recovered, three weeks later, I had a relapse. This time, the typhoid and malaria tests were positive.

Maybe it was God's way of saying I must do the show. If the tests had come out positive the first time, I would definitely have backed out! And I wouldn't have known the power of music and dance on the human body.

S. Meera

Bird's Eye

It all started when I took both my girls to the game section at a local mall in Ahmedabad. While they enjoyed their automated rides and air hockey, I was tempted to take up the challenge of a machine which dared me to ping it between 9.995 seconds to 10.005 seconds! Seemed fairly easy to me, and I did try twice, but I was horribly off the mark. I then waited patiently and observed others who also came with my confidence, only to be proved unworthy by the machine. In the major part of the hour that I spent there, I kept a watch on the game and not one person won the Toblerone or the other goodies hanging inside the encased glass shelf as prizes.

The next day, I read a story in which I came across a small bit of trivia—that it takes exactly one second to say the word 'chimpanzee'. I realised that if I could say chimpanzee ten times, within ten seconds, I'd fall within the time frame set by the machine! I borrowed my husband's sports watch and timed myself. I practised saying chimpanzee ten times and pressed the stop button as soon as I had finished saying it the last time. After about two days of practise, I was fairly confident of my skill and suggested that we go to the game park to entertain ourselves. 'Blow precious money on mindless video games, Mom,' mimicked my elder one. I smiled and we made our way to the game station once again.

I hit the button in the right time frame four times out of five. Not only did we scoop our Toblerones, but I even managed to take home the 'Hello Kitty' jackpot prize which could only be won if I could ping it precisely on the tenth second.

Soon enough came next week, and I promised them a hundred per cent strike rate. But to my horror, I goofed up four out of five times. As I introspected on what went wrong, I realised that when I was repeating the word 'chimpanzee', my mind was not just on the word, but on the thought that 'I am good at this', as against the previous visit when all I had thought of was the word chimpanzee and nothing else. That small deviation changed the rhythm and I goofed. When, on the last coin, I pushed every thought away, I got the button bang on 9.996 seconds.

When I went to the machine the next week with my five coins, I concentrated on not thinking of how good I had been ... yet again I lost on the time frame, because I was thinking of 'not thinking'. When I timed post 10.005 seconds, I thought that I should not drawl my 'chimpanzees' and so quickened the pace, thereby finishing my ten 'chimpanzees' when it was just about 9.80 seconds. When I timed in less than 9.995 seconds, I thought of how I should not hurry on my chimpanzees and I went back to drawling!

What had gone wrong with me, I wondered. What had been right the time I had won four out of five attempts, which I could not seem to replicate again?

It was then that I understood the story about Arjuna hitting the eye of the bird. In the first trip, I had thought of nothing except saying 'chimpanzee'—not of winning or losing, not feeling over-confident or under-confident. I just concentrated on the task at hand without the association of 'self' and the consequence of making/not making it on others. In the first trip, dissociation came naturally, for my ego had not stepped in. In all others, I was first me and then the game—naturally I lost!

Raksha Bharadia

Fighting Myself

Letters and notes in personal diaries have been preserved since a long time. Some of them give us an insight into the minds of great people like Mahatma Gandhi, while others help us by giving us an inside view of the problems an individual faced during a period of time, like Anne Frank.

Rakesh was a college student who loved playing cricket, watching *Dexter* on Cartoon Network and scary movies. But he was having serious problems in life. He wanted to pen down his thoughts too, just in case it might help someone, somewhere.

So Rakesh started writing a letter titled 'To Whomsoever It May Concern'. It began like this:

It was a Saturday night and all my friends were getting together. There would be everything that one could dream of, to forget about your worries—lip-smacking chicken tikka, to be followed by chocolate ice-cream, and a late night drive in the lovely winter weather. But today I was not in the mood. Since afternoon it had been hounding me. Pursuing me with all its might. I was scared. Scared for my life. Scared about my very sanity. All of a sudden, the thoughts enter my head and refuse to go away. Weird thoughts. Negative thoughts. Painful thoughts. Thoughts that you simply cannot share with other people. And then the rituals would begin. Washing my hands. Because no matter how much I washed them, they never felt clean. Praying again and again. Because sometimes I felt that I had not said that particular prayer properly. At other times it would be the tying of laces. And rechecking them. And then checking them again. And again.

Why me? The first question that comes to my mind on an everyday basis. Do people even have a problem like this? I mean, being stressed during exams is normal, not being able to understand your girlfriend is accepted nowadays, not brushing your teeth before sleeping is also not that uncommon, but what are all these thoughts that enter my head. And why do I have to repeat so many things? Why can't my problems be normal for a change? I would prefer skiing in the Himalayas with Big Foot instead of this any day.

Rakesh stopped writing for the day and went to sleep. But he wasn't the sort that gave up that easily. Beneath his stupid jokes, general clumsiness and the embarrassment that he faced regularly at the hands of others, lay a determined man. He would find a cure to this problem. He understood that, unlike other problems, this one was tricky as hell. It wasn't a physical predicament, but one that bothered him at the mental level. So he decided that the best way to defeat the enemy was to find out everything about it. And that's exactly what Rakesh did. As we find out in his next entry.

Googled my problem and found out that it goes by the name of Obsessive Compulsive Disorder (OCD). In short, it means that some of us get disturbing thoughts that refuse to go away, and to forget about them we start performing certain rituals. There are all kinds of stuff—washing of hands, praying again and again, being obsessive about cleanliness. The list can go on.

Apparently Cognitive Behaviour Therapy (CBT) helps in improving the patient. And this is something that is done under the guided supervision of a psychologist and also certain medicines are to be prescribed by a psychiatrist.

The entries to Rakesh's diary ended that day. He was in

deep conflict about visiting a psychologist and taking medicines. Which, a certain part of him said, he would probably have to do, as his compulsions were getting worse by the day, striking at any time of the day or night. He finally told his parents about these obsessions of his, and fortunately they supported him and lent a patient ear whenever the need arose. He felt better after confiding his fears to two of his best friends. And the fact that they accepted him the way he was, even after he had told them all those embarrassing things about himself, was immensely reassuring.

Everyday he would ask God why he was going through so disturbing a problem. And everyday he asked him for a way out of it. A few weeks later, and after suffering several tormented moments thanks to his problem, Rakesh came across an article about OCD in a magazine. That day, he noted down in his diary whatever he had read.

Here's the awesome thing: I'm not alone! There are loads of people out there with this dilemma. And the part that is most surprising is that a whole lot of celebrities have it! David Beckham has OCD. Priyanka Chopra has OCD. And last I heard, these guys were doing pretty well for themselves. David is raking in the moolah with his amazing football skills, and Priyanka is the new reigning queen of Bollywood.

Rakesh got in touch with a psychologist a few weeks later and met her. A few meetings later, it was decided that he had to start taking medication. And after several meetings with her, his knowledge of the predicament had become even better. He even started taking medication. But very, very reluctantly. Because to him, medication meant accepting defeat. Being dependent on external devices. He poured his heart out regarding these insecurities to his psychologist, who explained to him the importance of the medicines in a disorder like this, which is neuro-biological in nature.

Then the miracle happened. Slowly and steadily he noticed

that his compulsions were dying down, and he started going out more. Life began to show him colours that for so long he had been deprived of. The problems that he thought would haunt him to his grave had already started to disappear. After completing his course of medication, Rakesh gave up the medicines. Life had started to offer an endless amount of possibilities. Of course, there was always the chance that the problem could return, and he might go through hell again. But he would again try to stave off his fears and consult the people who had helped him.

Kabir Singh Bhandari

Following My Footsteps

'The best teachers teach from the heart, not from the book.'

—Author Unknown

About fifteen years back, I taught in a public school. The students belonged to various parts of the country and were from all levels of society.

I was the 4th grade teacher for science and maths. They were such a lovely set of children to be with. They were curious, asked endless questions and were eager to learn, which made teaching an absolute joy. I loved our lively discussions; they always made the lessons more interesting.

One of the girls in the class, Sapna, came from a poor family and I remember her as being a very hardworking and diligent child; eager to please, eager to learn.

She also happened to be handicapped. She had lost her fingers in a domestic accident while helping with daily chores.

One day, I happened to finish my class just before the lunch hour. I decided to stay back to go through my notes before heading to the staff-room. Suddenly, the solitary figure of Sapna caught my eye. . . .

I watched her struggle with her lunch-box. When she finally managed to open it, she sat there, all alone at her bench, and ate. None of the other students approached her to give her company or to share their lunch. It was as if they didn't notice her presence in their midst at all.

I realised that they were all probably apprehensive about her deformity and did not know how to deal with it. They thought she was different and didn't know how to approach her.

I realised that a lecture would not shake my students out of their apathy, no matter how innocent or misplaced. It would be of no use explaining to them the error of their actions, but at the same time, I didn't want them to shun the little girl, a fellow classmate, just because of her misfortune. But what could I do?

Then it came to me ... what if I taught by example?

As soon as this thought entered my head, I took my lunchbox, went and sat down next to Sapna and shared it with her. As I spoke to her and ate out of her box and offered her mine, the rest of the children in class, curious to know why the teacher was being especially friendly to this particular student, slowly inched forward. I called them all by name and shared my lunch as well as Sapna's. They all seemed to visibly relax and open up to her. They started to chat with her and, within minutes, became more comfortable and friendly with her. She reciprocated happily and won over her fellow classmates in no time at all.

They probably never truly understood why they should not treat her differently, but the important thing that day was that they accepted her as she was.

I don't know what kind of impact I had on those children, but it was one of those moments which stirred me greatly and made me thank God yet again, for giving me the opportunity to be in such a wonderful profession that allowed me to mould hundreds of beautiful, young, impressionable minds. And then to watch those minds bloom, blossom and spread their fragrance of joy, innocence and exuberance.

Sayli Deshmukh

Going to the Roots

This happened many years back. My son-in-law entrusted me with rupees three lakh to buy him a flat in Delhi. When I explored the market, I found that nothing good was available for less than five to six lakh rupees. He told me to keep the cash with the promise that he would send the rest of the amount soon.

The money lay idle with me for a few months. It was then that a friend who was also a chartered accountant visited us and suggested that I put the amount on interest. The idea appealed to me and I did put it on interest, through my friend, for a three-month period. I started receiving the interest money every month and was very glad with my decision. But after about six months or so, this friend stopped giving me the interest money. When I tried contacting him, I got no response. He never came on the phone when I called nor returned any of my calls. He would either be in a meeting, a shower or eating his meal. About three months went by this way, and with each passing day my agitation and anxiety grew.

Around the same time, my son-in-law called to say he was sending the rest of the money, and that I should start the registration process. I found myself in a terrible fix. I did not have the money. It was a prodigious amount and I simply did not have it.

I became angry, irritable and extremely negative. I lost sleep, worrying about all that my son-in-law would think of me. More than anything, I hated the man who had brought me to such a state. I harboured thoughts of harming him, getting him arrested, hitting him—anything that would make him suffer as I was. My mind then was full of revenge, no positivity came from anywhere. Truly, I was a wreck in those days.

During one such anxiety-ridden night, I was once again riding on the negative train of thoughts with sleep eluding me completely. Tired and irritable, I got up from the bed to fetch myself a glass of water. When I returned to my bed, I saw a book by Osho lying on the side table. I opened it at a random page and started reading. After reading about a page, a sentence came which transformed my perspective totally. It said that, in our life, whenever we face a trying situation or a problem, we must look within for its root cause, for that is where the problem owes its existence, and that is also from where the solution will come. I remember reading that line over and over again—at least twenty-five times if not more. After which I closed the book and started pondering on it in relation to my situation.

I understood everything. I realised that it was my decision to part with the amount in the hope of earning a few extra bucks. My friend had not forced me into it, he had merely suggested it. I was the one who was lured by the profit and for the six months that I did receive the interest, I complimented myself on my smartness. But when the money was lost, I was quick to push the blame on him. In the middle of the night, my mind exploded with this realisation: that my irritation, anger, frustration was the result of my wrongdoing, not my friend's. Along with this, my anger and frustration vanished too! Then and there I decided to change my focus. Henceforth I would stop ruminating on the loss and concentrate on earning the money so that I could hand it over to the rightful owner. Which I did.

Interestingly, I bumped into the friend in a restaurant after about two years of this entire fiasco. He came up to me and apologised for his behaviour, saying that he was embarrassed about what had happened and that he was aware that he had to return the money. I told him he should not worry about it and that he could give it to me whenever he was able to do so conveniently. I said this with all my heart, for I held nothing against him.

Even today, that line which came to me from Osho guides me. I live in a big joint family, where we do happen to have conflicting views and differences of opinion. I always look within myself in every problem and try and find out where I went wrong. Once I understand it, I just need to put things right!

Rajan Mishra
(As told to Amita Dalal)

Just a Little Patience

I was eight years old, and nothing seemed more wonderful than taking balls of multi-coloured wool and creating fantastic garments out of them. I asked my grandmother to teach me to knit, and though my mother told her I was too young to learn, my grandmother saw no reason why I could not try.

Learning to hold the needles was easy, as was slipping on the first stitch. After that, I hit a blank wall.

'Patience,' my grandmother warned me, when after my seventy-fifth unsuccessful attempt at pushing the needle through the stitch, wrapping the wool around the needle, drawing the wool in and slipping the old stitch off, I was ready to throw the pair of knitting needles out of the window. 'Knitting is a skill you learn for life. You can't rush it.'

To be honest, after all these years, I am not sure if those were her exact words, but there was no ambiguity in the tone of her voice.

'Patience,' I muttered to myself, as I tried again.

If it were a story, I would have been successful in knitting my first stitch, but since this is not a story, I did not succeed that time either. But I kept at it, and a few days later, I finally got it. Within a week, I was making knit stitches almost effortlessly. Learning to 'purl' was much easier than it had been to learn to 'knit', and before I knew it, a whole world of patterns had been laid open for me. Long before my tenth birthday, I could follow any pattern in the book, and even my grandmother's friends had started asking me to help them with the more complicated knitting patterns.

I never kept at it, though, and most of my adult life has been free of knitting needles and wool. But my grandmother was right. Knitting is a skill I've never forgotten. My tension remains inconsistent—sometimes my stitches are so tight, I can barely push the needle through, other times they are so loose, sunlight could stream through the gaps—reflecting my current mood. But there is no pattern I cannot tackle, no garment I cannot do.

And yet, none of it would have happened had my grandmother not whispered that magic word in my ear—Patience.

In life, as in knitting, the only thing we need to succeed is patience. Genuine patience.

Rayna Talwar

Lessons from a Parking Lot Attendant

'Sir! Five rupees,' said an old, quavering voice from behind. I was in Erode, Tamil Nadu. Crazy about temples, I had decided to visit the famous Arudra Kapaleeswarar temple, in the heart of the city. My taxi was parked outside as I went in, had a holy tête-à-tête with the Creator and walked out with my hands full of prasad and heart full of contentment.

His demand for the parking fee was an unwelcome intrusion and, irritated, I struggled to fish out the money from my wallet. It was difficult as both my hands were full. This further irritated me, and I looked at him balefully. He must have been around eighty years old, wore a soiled dhoti and was barefoot.

As he extended his wrinkled hands, I saw he was trembling. I noticed that he was probably malnourished—I could practically count the ribs on his bare chest.

My heart went out to him then, and I took out ten rupees. He promptly paid me the balance and would not entertain my entreaties that he keep the change. He then proceeded to pull out a dilapidated book, tore a token from it and gave it to me.

I knew that if I took the token, he would have to pay the authorities, who probably gave him a meagre salary for this job. I told him to keep the token. I even suggested that he have bun and tea with the money.

He vigorously shook his head and said, 'No, sir! I do not want to cheat the government, and that too in front of the temple.' He thrust the token into my hands.

I was left gaping as he trudged away, flabbergasted at his sense of independence and his work ethic. Here was an old man for whom five rupees would have meant the world and yet, in spite of his poverty, he put his work ethics before his needs.

I learnt a few lessons that day. I learnt that it is more respectable to be independent. I learnt that honesty is still the best policy. I learnt that education, ethics and personality need not necessarily go together. I learnt that one should be thankful for all that one has. Many are not as privileged.

I may not meet the old man again, but those weary eyes will always be a motivation for me.

Komal Venkataraman

Losing the Battle to Win the War

It was the final round of the selections for our school elocution competition. I was eleven and competing to represent Ashlin House in the finals, just as I had done the previous year.

Someone called my name and it was my turn to get onto the stage. I could feel my heart beating faster and all my stomach muscles tightening up. I announced the poem to the audience, '*Lochinvar* by Sir Walter Scott.'

Then, mysteriously, the fear melted away, and I lost myself in the re-telling of the ancient Scottish ballad that had grown to be my own. As I ended to thunderous applause, I knew that I had done well.

The rest of the afternoon was a blur and a mere formality. I was only waiting to hear my name announced amongst the finalists.

The judges debated the results and then Miss Inayat came on stage with a piece of paper in her hand. She announced the finalists for Kinnaird and Wellingdon house. I waited as my turn approached.

'Ashlin House will be represented by—'

'Christina, Christina, Christina,' the audience changed.

'—Delnaz Ravji.'

For a minute, there was pin-drop silence. I was not sure if I had heard correctly. Then Miss Inayat continued, 'I know that some of you feel that it should be Christina. But she moved her body too much on stage. An elocution competition is about only using facial expressions.'

I had never felt so completely shattered. I had been the best that day. I knew that. But for some reason, that hadn't been enough.

I tried to put it behind me, saying that there would be another time. But two years later, when I changed schools and cities, I left without winning another elocution competition or representing Ashlin House again.

My new school did not emphasise extracurricular activities and I did not think that I would participate in another elocution. But then one day, I chanced to hear about an upcoming interschool competition. On a whim, I entered my name for it.

Once more I found myself turning to *Lochinvar* to beat the competition and win the right to represent my school. But I finally decided that I could do with a more sophisticated piece. After all, *Lochinvar* was for children.

So, I selected John F. Kennedy's inaugural address and, much practice later, I was at the finals of the eagerly-awaited interschool competition. As the other contestants recited their pieces, I knew in my heart that JFK would not win this competition for me.

As I walked up the stairs to the stage, I made up my mind. '*Lochinvar* by Sir Walter Scott,' I told the audience. Then, in my mind, I was eleven again and competing for the right to represent Ashlin House.

As the last syllable left my lips, I knew that I had given it my all. I would probably never be better than I was that day.

I heard the applause in the distance. It slowly dawned on me that I had finished. Winning no longer mattered. I bowed and left the auditorium. The next day a friend brought me the results. Yes, I had won the interschool competition.

I did not know it then, but among the audience was a girl who would be my class representative three years later in college. She never forgot *Lochinvar*. She also remembered me. So it happened, that on her insistence, I represented my class for the college elocution competition.

I won. Three years in a row.

It also followed that I represented the college elocution and debating team through my time in college. Here also began my interest in drama. Together, this contributed to making my college life an unforgettable experience.

Through all of it, I continued to shake a lot on stage. Strangely, no one seemed to mind very much. I guess that's what they call finding your own style!

I had lost in my attempt to represent Ashlin House when I was eleven. But the hard work that I put in stood me in good stead over the next decade.

Sometimes, you must lose the battle to win the war. I also believe that everything is connected.

Christina Daniels

My Recollections of Mountaineering

The following extract is from the personal memoirs of my grandfather, Colonel Autar Singh Cheema. Though I never met him, I have heard he was a great human being who was humble and believed that actions spoke louder than words. It is an unpublicised fact that he was the first Indian, the first Army officer, and the first paratrooper to set foot on top Mount Everest. To accomplish this great challenge without any formal training, and in a short span of one year, is a feat which no one can beat.

*

People have often asked me how I managed to climb Everest. My reply has always been that I never was a mountaineer but this opportunity just came my way. I had never done any mountaineering course, basic or advance. I had not gone on any expedition either. It was just a sequence of events in the drama of my life.

In September '61, we joined the battalion at Agra—the Mecca of paratroopers. By the end of the year, there was some activity and we spent six months in Goa as the occupation force. After this, we got back to Agra. Life was lethargic and monotonous for the youngsters there. Fortunately, I got a break. There was a telegram from the

Indian Mountaineering Foundation (IMF) asking whether I would be willing to join an expedition to Panch-Chuli. I was thrilled and ran around showing the telegram to my friends and then to the second-in-command with an application in my hand requesting for annual leave (without knowing that I could have been detailed on duty). The leave application was turned down by the commanding officer (CO), who said he did not want any gladiators in the unit. I was a disappointed man, and did not reply to the telegram. One fine afternoon, in protest, all the youngsters got together at the mess and happened to receive a call from the IMF. They did not hesitate to inform the IMF that the CO was not keen to oblige. The secretary of the IMF, H.C. Sarin, promptly sent a message stating, 'If Cheema is keen to join the expedition he should report to the GSO 2 MS Branch by 0900hrs 20 April '64. The signal would follow the next day.' Off I went the next day, but not before giving a certificate stating that I was willing to forego my annual leave.

The members of the Panch-Chuli expedition had already collected in Delhi. Preparations were in full swing. They all knew each other and were talking of various mountaineering feats, developments in the equipment, capabilities of individual sherpas, how the previous six expeditions had failed on this mountain, strategy of climbing and so on. I was ignorant about all this and did not even know the whereabouts of this famous Panch-Chuli massif. The leader realised my weakness and I was not entrusted with any job worth the name. We moved out of Delhi and on reaching the end of the road had to employ the porters. This is where I stepped in. Because of all my experience in man-management through commanding a rifle company, I was given charge of the porters. I did my duty sincerely, actively and honestly. Not a single porter could move without my permission. In the cover of darkness and away from the base camp site, I started learning how to use climbing ropes, ice axes, pitons, etc. from my sherpa, Lobsung.

We started with negotiating the difficult rocky and ice slopes, preparing the way and establishing inter-mediatory camps. For the first ferry to camp one, two ropes of one member and one sherpa each were detailed to haul up the stores. We went without crampons. The leader of the second rope was an experienced climber, who like a matured mountaineer, did not want to take undue risks. So on a couple of difficult and dangerous pitches, he wanted to return to the base camp in order to move up the next day with better aids to negotiate the same with better climbing techniques. Our rope, on the expert and courageous advice of Lobsung, trudged along till we reached the site of camp one and perforce the other rope had to follow us. On our return to the base camp, the entire lot was briefed that young Cheema was a bachelor, a paratrooper and a skier who would kill himself and his rope-mate, taking undue risks. So half the battle was won; then onwards, Lobsung and I prepared the route to each and every camp till we climbed two virgin peaks, Peak 5 (21,120 ft) and Peak 4 (20,840 ft) of the Panch-Chuli massif—*in one day*. On our way back, we had lunch at one of the restaurants at Nainital. There was an *Indian Express* newspaper lying on the table in front of us with a photograph of a climber with the caption 'Cheema climbs two virgin peaks of Panch-Chuli in one day'. I became a mountaineer overnight.

Some senior officers apparently said that, if this chap had to burn his face, why did he go all the way to the Himalayas. He could have achieved the same by sitting in front of the fireplace or facing the Agra mid-day sun in June. That was the level of motivation from some seniors!

Once again a letter came asking for my willingness to participate in the pre-Everest expedition planned for Rathong

Peak in Sikkim Himalayas. I was allowed to go, but only after receiving a posting order which asked me to report to a new raising. On the pre-Everest expedition, we met the most renowned mountaineers at Darjeeling, some of whom had already been to Everest a couple of times.

On our return to Darjeeling, after scaling the peak, the president and secretary of IMF arrived to make the final selection for the 1965 Everest team in consultation with the principal and designate leader and deputy leader of the team. Before the final announcement of the team, a cocktail party was thrown by the principal. A lot of Scotch was consumed by mountaineers like me who had hardly any hopes of being included in the team. When the names were announced, somebody lifted me up from the back and congratulated me for being selected. When I looked back, it was none other than the famous Everest climber Shri Tenzing Norgay! The rest is history.

Gunit Locham

Sight Beyond Vision

I had my first brush with the world of the blind at age nine, when a blind man came to our house to repair our broken chairs. He walked several miles everyday, and what I found most amazing about him was his surefootedness and his pace. In the bitter, dry winter of north Indian plains, he would work almost non-stop with his chafed and occasionally bleeding fingers; running them deftly over the tiny holes in the frame of the chairs, ensuring that the needle pulling the nylon thread never missed a single hole. Curious to know more about wood, he once asked me what a tree looked like. I got past the general shape, trunk, branches and leaves easily, but got stuck at the colour green! I am not sure what was more annoying to me: his incomprehension of the concept of colour or my inability to describe it. But to my child's mind, it was a frustrating deadlock.

Nine years later, I met the only blind person I can call a close friend and the one who left a lasting impression on me about blindness. A strange rule of the university had brought us together. An MA final student in arts, he could only get a 'writer' for his exams from the science faculty. A mutual friend asked me to help him prepare for his exams and also be his official writer. We lived in the same hostel and the first time I went to his room I blabbered insensitively, 'Why is it so dark in here, why is the light turned off? I was about to leave, thinking you were not in yet.' To which he genially replied, 'Sorry, friend, now that you are here I will turn it on for you, it doesn't make a difference to me.'

The three months that I spent with him taught me so much about the blind. I realised how difficult it is to prepare for an exam when someone else has to do the reading (only a few of the books he needed were in Braille). Completing a chapter felt like running a marathon.

I also got a taste of his pride. He would insist on making tea for us, plugging in the thick aluminium wires himself, often getting an electric shock in the process. He wouldn't let me light his cigarette, even though his fingers and parts of his nose and lips sometimes got burnt in the process.

Exams were a nervous time, more for me than him. While I read the question paper again and again, he would patiently light a cigarette and marshal his thoughts for what seemed like an eternity. By this time, more than thirty minutes would have passed, and that was all the grace he was allowed by the university for his blindness. Last I heard, he had got a job and he got married too. His wife, too, was blind.

A few years ago, I had to rush to attend to my mother who had suffered a heart attack. Unable to get a confirmed seat on the train, I decided to travel in a general compartment. By paying a coolie, I got an aisle seat in a coach that was packed like sardines. The section behind mine was occupied by a noisy group of boys whose decibel level was higher than that of the clacking of the train on its tracks. It was really hot, stuffy, noisy and crowded in there, and to make matters worse, there was no light in the compartment and I could not see a thing around me.

Among film stories, popular heroines, some unknown girls, politics and stories of earlier travels, what caught my attention was a heated exchange on the game of cricket among the boys, which went something like this:

Boy One: They could not play my bowling.

Boy Two: But we didn't win because of your bowling, it was my performance with the bat that saw us home.

Boy Three: And what about the catch I took to dismiss their star batsman?

Boy Four: And my sixer when the asking rate was high? No one mentions that.

Their teacher: Hey you boys! Are you going to spend the night fighting?

Ignoring their teacher, they continued to bicker and argue. They were also playing with what sounded like a pair of cymbals, the kind used in temples, which was really annoying as they kept throwing it around and hitting each other with it. Once or twice it came very close to me. Then it hit me on my shoulder and just as I turned around to give them a piece of my mind on making so much racket in the dead of the night, the lights came on. What I saw before me was something I had not expected. There must have been fifteen or twenty teenaged boys. They were all blind.

I looked at the thing that had hit me. It was a ball that blind cricketers use. Without saying a word, I returned it to their teacher, the only member of their team who could see. He saw it all on my face. Must have been used to it. He said with finality, 'All right, everyone go to sleep now, we have a match tomorrow.' Needless to say, I didn't sleep the whole night and thanked the Lord for His gift and what I had seen with it.

Piyush Panwar

The Edge

Have you ever lived on the edge?
gulping down fear
trying hard to not look beyond
or smell the blood from your cracked feet
to keep your footing on the slippery rim
Scanning the horizon
for a careless jostle, the shove
that could send you tumbling?

One day I jumped off the edge
and discovered
there was no below.

Alaka Yeravadekar

The Indomitable Soldier

At seventy-six, Lt. Col. Surindar Sawhney (Retd) packs in a busy day. In the morning and evening, he helps his daughter Harleen run Cherry-On-The-Top—her highly successful bakery-catering-coffee-shop in Pune. But the day is not just about work, for he also takes time out to play golf and pack in a few games of bridge.

You would never guess that Lt. Col. Sawhney uses an artificial leg. Not from the way he weaves his Kinetic in and out of Pune's rush-hour traffic, not from the way he guns his car down the national highway as he takes his family for a vacation, not from the way he punches a drive down a golf course, and certainly not from the way he walks—straight, firm and tall.

The ramrod straight back, the trim figure, the firm handshake all bespeak the sturdy soldier. But this doughty war-veteran knows all too well the trauma of losing a leg to a landmine during the Indo–Pak War of 1965.

A Bombay Sapper, he recalls those turbulent times when he was still a major, 'I was commanding a forward post in the Rann of Kutch, where our duties included the dangerous work of clearing minefields. In one particular area, we were sure that there was a mine under the ground, but even after trying for a long time, my havildar couldn't locate it. I told him to step back while I carefully went over to stand exactly where he had placed his feet (in a minefield, one has to be extremely careful where one steps, because one wrong move can set off a mine hidden below). Finding nothing unusual, I asked him to hand over the mine-detector to me, swivelling my right foot about forty-five degrees as I held out my hand.'

The next moment a massive explosion rent the air. That tiny fraction of a movement was enough to trigger off the mine, buried directly below in the sand. Bleeding profusely and in acute pain, the brave soldier had to wait half an hour for a helicopter to evacuate him to the field hospital. There, while the sounds of battle raged all around them, in a makeshift surgery deep inside a bunker, his right leg was amputated.

He was then brought to the Artificial Limb Centre in Pune, where to the amazement of the doctors, his wound healed within a week. But further surgeries were required to make the amputated part ready to accept an artificial limb. There was soreness, there was pain, and the adjustment of learning to walk again with this new extension. But the indomitable soldier did not falter.

'I had resolved from the first day that I would not use a walking stick,' he states firmly. He began to practise intensively with the new limb. Within six months, he purchased a second-hand car and learnt to drive it using only the left foot. Another few months, and he was riding his faithful old scooter.

But while the physical healing was quick, the mental trauma took longer. He had always been a champion sportsman. At the National Defence Academy, he had passed out with multiple honours—as Academy Cadet Captain, as a silver medallist, as well as swimming and tennis blues. At the Indian Military Academy too, he had received the coveted gold medal and more tennis honours.

But with tennis now out of reach because of his handicap, he seethed with hidden anger. For five years, he nursed his resentment and would not even watch a game.

It was wife Indira's patient encouragement which gradually changed his views. 'She had just given birth to our second daughter Harleen, who was diagnosed with a rare birth defect called epidermolysis bullosa. Harleen's skin is so fragile and thin, that she bleeds at the slightest touch. Indira had to constantly be at her side for all her needs, handling her as lightly as possible. I realised that she was the one who faced the maximum trauma—with me in hospital, an uncertain future, and two little daughters to look after. And she did it all with amazing serenity and without ever losing her cool.'

Gradually, Lt. Col. Sawhney came to terms with his disability. He also realised that the disability, which would hamper active service, required a change of focus. He branched off into data processing, becoming one of the first military men to specialise in computers in those early days in the '60s.

How did he cope with the trauma? He sums it up in two simple words—'family and prayer'. 'It was a sense of togetherness. I felt that, as a family, we could cope with everything and anything. Even now, I pray every morning for an hour—it gives me immeasurable strength. I always thank God for all the good things in life that he has given me.'

Indira says simply, 'God has blessed us with inner strength to face the pressure. We never felt that we could not cope, neither did my husband indulge in self-pity.'

Their positive attitude is reflected in their words of gratitude for the friends and colleagues who rallied around them and helped him regain his equanimity. 'First of all, there was Brigadier Jenkins, a World War II amputee and a recipient of the Military Cross who constantly gave me words of encouragement. My fellow officers and friends visited me regularly at the hospital. Every Friday without fail, the wife of my commandant would send me a lovely bouquet of roses in order to cheer me up. I remember that once (for some reason) it did not arrive, and the nurse kidded me, "What Major, no one loves you anymore?" and she went out, plucked some fresh flowers from the hospital garden and arranged them in my vase. People were so caring.'

Having received so much care, Lt. Col. Sawhney feels that he too must give back to others in a similar predicament. He regularly visits the Artificial Limb Centre to meet the present lot of amputee soldiers who come in for fittings of artificial limbs, and offers them words of encouragement and solace.

'I tell them what another officer told me—I know what you must be feeling. But don't think about what you have lost, concentrate on what you have.'

And that is his guiding principle in life—even after losing so much, he feels that he has gained much more.

Mita Banerjee

The Moment You Wish ...

The height of your accomplishments will equal the depth of your convictions.

—William F. Scolavino

My family has been associated with music since the last three hundred years, and everyone wanted the two of us to be musicians. We had unconditional support from our parents. Their advice to us was simple: 'Concentrate on your riyaaz, God will be behind you in everything.'

But in those days, it was not easy to sustain oneself only on an income from music. I had to take up a job to sustain my family and myself. I worked for about ten months in all. Even during those ten months, I knew that this was not what I was meant for. I was meant for music. I also understood that my only choice in life was to give my all to my love. But I still needed a helping hand, that minimum amount of money without which I could not have surrendered my day to what I was most passionate about.

The opportunity came to me sooner rather than later. During my service days, a concert was held in Delhi during the Saboo Pratap Singh Memorial festival. An artist who was supposed to participate in it took ill and I was sent to be his replacement. That concert was the turning point of my life. Jagjit Singh sahib happened to be in the audience and was impressed with my talent. He summoned me after the concert and asked about my whereabouts. I narrated my situation. He offered to give me the amount which I earned in my job as stipend money, and asked whether I would then surrender myself fully to the music world.

Since then, I firmly believe that if you have a goal and are honest and sincere towards it, God gives you an opportunity to make it happen. If one has single-minded focus, all the powers in the world come together to help you realise that goal. In my case God sent Jagjit sahib as my saviour. I truly believe that it is our thoughts, our karma, which eventually become our destiny. God then has to come and help us in our endeavour, for God is within us—God is within each of us. The important thing is to dream, and then work and give it one's all!

Rajan Saajan Mishra
(As told to Amita Dalal)

The Next Best Thing

I met Sidharth Sharma as part of a series of interviews I conducted with corporate honchos, through my stint with Radio City 91.1 FM as a radio jockey.

When I first met Sidharth, founder and chief operating officer of Foundations PR, I did not know what to expect. I was a little apprehensive of what I should or should not speak to him about. Trying to be sensitive of how he would react and how I should broach the subject of his disability. How would I make a reference to him being blind? Possibly the only blind person in the world heading a public relations company! But when I finally met him, it was a totally different scenario. In most of my interactions with company heads, it's me trying to make things comfortable and relaxed before the actual interview (media can probably unnerve the coolest of corporate honchos, or perhaps it's just me!), but with Sidharth there was a role reversal. He walked in, dressed smartly, and with a cool sense of confidence. Had it not been for the hint of support he sought from his colleague while walking, one could never have guessed about his visual handicap. Through the greetings, it almost felt like he sensed my discomfort; immediately he took on the task of making me feel at ease. The rest was smooth flowing, in bits I sometimes felt like he was the one driving the show!

Through the interaction, I discovered, to my pleasant

surprise, that Sidharth not once used his disability as an excuse. He had climbed the corporate ladder progressively with each successful assignment. Alongside, he continually challenged ... well, his challenge. From conquering mountain peaks to leading expeditions and organising the cricket world cup for the blind. His unfaltering enthusiasm was encouraging. The bike accident that had caused him to lose his vision at twenty-four had not robbed him of his indomitable spirit. When I asked him if he had been shattered at the moment of truth, his emphatic reply was, 'No! I just looked forward to the next best thing.'

At the time of the accident, Sidharth was preparing to get married to his girlfriend of seven years. The preparations were under way, but post the accident, understandably, the marriage was deferred. Sidharth's relationship with his girlfriend continued and slowly a year went past. With each passing month, failed attempts to restore Sidharth's eyesight also went by. By the end of the year, it was quite certainly determined that the damaged optic nerves in Sidharth's eyes could never be repaired. The parents of the girl by then were unwilling for the relationship to continue. Tantrums were thrown by the father with an ailing heart and guilt trips feigned by the extended aunts and uncles. Sidharth could see through all of this and finally decided to call off the relationship. That day he said, 'I realised for the first time that I had been robbed of something very, very precious. We both howled in each other's arms and I knew this was it.' The girl subsequently got married to someone else and Sidharth moved on to accomplish his professional endeavours.

The interview with Siddharth is long over, but the impression he created will last for a while. My own positive attitude and never say die spirit seemed to have found resonance in Sidharth's story. And with each unsolicited jerk life may impose, my vision is set on the next best thing.

Suparnaa Chadda

3

BE THE CHANGE

No kind action ever stops with itself. One kind action leads to another. Good example is followed. A single act of kindness throws out roots in all directions, and the roots spring up and make new trees. The greatest work that kindness does to others is that it makes them kind themselves.

—Amelia Earhart

A Glimmer of Hope

It was Friday, 5 June 2009. At around 3 p.m., I drove my Ford Ikon into 80 Feet Road in Indiranagar in Bangalore, heading for a meeting with a client. As I entered the wide road, I saw a posse of traffic constables who stopped my car on the side and asked me to produce my car documents to the traffic sub-inspector (SI) who was standing on the footpath. I walked up to the SI and showed him my driving licence. He then asked me to show him my car insurance certificate and pollution emission certificate. I walked back to my car and realised that I was not carrying either document. Cursing myself for such a slip, I apologised to the SI and asked what needed to be done. A half smile came upon his lips and he told me that the fine for not carrying the two documents was Rs 600, but I could pay him Rs 300. I took out my wallet and told the SI that I would pay the fine and he could issue me a receipt for the same. The SI suddenly grew hostile and in a stern voice told me that the fine would then be Rs 1,100. I paid him Rs 1,100 and took the receipt, wondering why the fine had suddenly escalated just because I wanted a receipt instead of paying the Rs 300 bribe for which he'd asked.

As I was driving back home after the meeting, I found myself angry as well as irritated over what had happened: with myself for not carrying the documents, and with the SI for blatantly demanding a bribe. When I reached my home, I logged on to the internet and found out that the traffic police of Bangalore had a website, which gave details of the chargeable fines. It also had a page for logging complaints, with the email id of the additional commissioner of police (ACP) for the traffic division. I wrote an email to the ACP, narrating what had happened. I copied the Lok Ayukta in on the message. Once I had sent the mail I felt better, since I thought I had played my role as a diligent citizen.

The next day, at about 2 p.m., I logged into my email and found three messages from the ACP! The first informed me that I had done the right thing by paying the fine and not the bribe, the second mail asked that I submit my complaint in writing and fax it to the ACP (which was necessary for action to be initiated against the SI), the third mail carried the ACP's direct numbers (and his cell number too) and a request that I call him so that he could personally follow-up with me as well.

On 8 June, I received a mail from the ACP stating that the erring SI had been suspended from services. I called him to thank him for his prompt action and to ask if anything more was required of me. He introduced himself and thanked me for doing what I did! He said that several Bangaloreans brought cases to him but backed out when asked to give the complaint in writing. He also apologised to me, saying he was sorry that somebody from his department had tried to bribe me and also harassed me, for the SI in fact did not have any business stopping me and asking for my documents since I had not committed any traffic violations. He invited me for tea at his office too.

After I kept the phone down, I could not believe that, within forty-eight hours of having asked for a bribe, the erring officer had been suspended. I wanted to meet the person who had, in a short ten-minute conversation, changed my notions of public services officers. I sought an appointment with him, and a few days later visited him in his office. I reached his office early and was immediately ushered into his cabin where I waited till he finished his meeting with a previous delegation. Precisely at 4.30 p.m. he ended his meeting and turned to me, spending the next twenty minutes discussing several aspects of traffic policing in Bangalore. Of course I got my cup of tea too (many corporate clients I visit do not see me on time and do not ask me for a cup of tea!).

As I was leaving the ACP's office, I told him, 'Over the years many of my friends and cousins have urged me to migrate and settle in one of the western countries, but I have consciously chosen to stay back in India. When I have interactions like the one I had with you Sir, I am happy that I made the choice to stay back in India.' It was an impromptu comment, straight from my heart, to which the ACP just smiled and shook my hand.

When I was walking out of the ACP's office, I felt reassured that if we have officers like him in our country, there is a glimmer of hope against corruption, provided we as citizens have the courage to say no to bribes, and have the inclination to report cases of bribe (I am no major social activist, yet I found all the information I needed on the web).

And, of course, Gandhiji's words came to my mind, 'Be the change you wish to see in the world'. I realised change begins with me, and I *can* make a difference!

Shabbir Merchant

A Hundred and Twenty-Five Rupees

The year was 1999, the place Surat. The Ganesh Visarjan procession was underway amidst loud dholak beats and cheer. I could see lakhs of heads chanting *Ganpati baba Moriya*, their faces smeared with red gulaal. Roads were choked with people carrying their idols for immersion in the river. As the additional commissioner of police, I was in charge of maintaining peace and order in that frightening mass where even a little panic could cause stampedes, leading to death and injury in hundreds. Under our watchful eye, the procession seemed to be moving ahead calmly.

The situation was tense because, in another part of the city, a smaller procession had turned violent owing to a dispute over the route and police had had to open fire, resulting in civilian casualties. This news could have far-reaching implications in the area where I was managing law and order. I had to ensure that nothing happened to inflame the already tense situation. It was like sitting on a keg of gunpowder. We were counting every minute that passed.

I checked my watch: another hour to go. I sent my men out to keep a check on any newcomer who might have information about the other procession. Thankfully, cell phones were not much in vogue in those days and we crossed our fingers for the time to pass quickly.

Suddenly one of my men came running to me and told me that a local newspaper had published news of the mishap as a special mid-day supplement, and a vendor had arrived with a stack of the same. Thankfully one of the hawaldars had caught notice of the man and he had been detained by our force. I went up to him and saw the provocative headlines. Those printed words to me then seemed no less than death incarnate, for there was no telling how the tightly-packed crowd would behave once they read the news.

I realised that the only way for me was to stop the distribution of the newspaper. But doing so was not a legally viable option. For a moment I struggled with the paradox of my situation and then the idea came like a wave!

I asked him the price of one supplement.

'One rupee sahib,' he said.

'How many do you have?' I asked.

'A hundred and twenty-five copies,' he answered.

I extracted the money and bought the entire stock of his merchandise. One hawaldar took him for tea and the procession carried on peacefully without a clue of what had happened. I sent a few of my men to other areas along the procession's route, instructing them to buy the entire stock of the newspaper, if they found it at a vendor.

Such an easy solution to a situation that could have turned ugly!

That night was one that I slept very peacefully.

H.P. *Singh*

Be a Troubleshooter

Once we were working on a large project, at an investment of Rs 40 crore, to make dextrose (obtained from maize). We recruited a person with a PhD in chemistry with a few years' experience—let us call him Dr Saha—as the chief executive.

Some of our licensing aspects were handled by a government office based in Mehsana, a city about sixty kilometres north of Ahmedabad. I asked Dr Saha to go to that office, meet a certain person who was processing our file, and get a letter—called NOC—that would enable us to proceed further with the project. All formalities had been completed, and with this letter—which we were told was ready—we could start our work.

That night, I waited to hear from him. But he neither called me that night, nor did he meet me the next morning. Around 11.30 a.m., I called him to my room and asked him for an update. He informed me that the person he was to meet was on leave. That's all! I said if that were the case, why hadn't he informed me on the phone. He had nothing to say. I said, I could have guided you on what to do next. Someone else could have issued the letter, had he checked? Why hadn't he updated me this morning? Didn't he realise that some parts of the project were being held up due to this letter? Still, he had nothing to say.

I called another colleague, Rajiv Mehta, and instructed him to go to Mehsana and get that letter. Next day, Rajiv went and called me late in the night, informing me that he had got the letter. He also said that he would tell me how he got it on reaching the office the next day.

The next morning, I called Dr Saha and Rajiv to my room. Rajiv gave me the letter and then narrated how he had obtained it:

I went to Mehsana; that man (Bachubhai) was on leave, as Dr Saha has already told you. I got his address from a colleague. When I explained why I was looking for Bachubai, another officer said he had the letter with him, but that Bachubhai had to sign it. So I requested that someone accompany me in my jeep with the official rubber stamp. An officer agreed (after some persuasion, of course, and explanation as to how the absence of the letter was holding up a large project, which will come up in their district and so give employment and economic benefits). He instructed a peon to accompany me and gave him the stamp, the stamp pad, and a file with the letter.

When we went to the house, Bachubhai was not there. We were told that he had gone out of town for a wedding and would be back after a few days. I found out the town he was in—which was about an hour away. So we went there!

But when we reached, the wedding party had already left on procession. We found the village they had gone to—which was about half an hour away—and found the place where the wedding was going on. Now the challenge was to find this person! We had to ask around quite a bit before we finally found Bachubhai. I introduced myself, explained the whole story to him, about our need for the letter as well as how much effort it had taken to trace him. I also stressed on the importance of the project for the district. He was very impressed and readily agreed to sign it. He even apologised for giving me so much trouble! He signed the letter, then I dropped the peon at Mehsana, reached home at nine in the night and then telephoned you. And sir, now the whole office is our friend. Any time we need anything done, no problem at all!

I got up from my chair and hugged Rajiv! I believe that one must not find reasons for not doing something, but ways to solve problems and move ahead. Evidently, Rajiv believed in this too.

Sunil Handa

David

I met David for the first time during a Caferati (a writer's forum) meet. We had corresponded earlier over mail—leaving comments or suggestions on each other's write-ups. David, who is an American, has been in India for over a year studying Indian classical music under the Gundecha brothers from Bhopal, Ramakant and Umakant Gundecha. He is also training in sarangi, under Sarwar Hussein, who resides in Bhopal as well. Besides these, he also received lessons in the rare instrument called vichitra vina, from the Baroda-based teacher, Smt. Radhika Budhkar.

You would think that David is essentially into music. Well, he chucked up his twenty-year career in a US law firm to pursue his passions. And his passions are not just confined to music. He has a great love for poetry and enjoys painting too!

David mesmerised us with his amazing rendition of a ghazal. It was doubly amazing as it was conceived and rendered in English while being faithful to its Urdu style and structure. Perhaps for all of us, it was a novel experience. Coming through him, the words felt like silk; smooth and soft, we all lost ourselves somewhere in its seductive and soothing folds.

A few lines from him:

> Irrational joy! ... my desire for sending you ghazals
> One's actually toying with fire ... when sending you ghazals
> The weight of my utterance deepens ... does gold feel this heavy?
> It's weird how my arm doesn't tire ... when sending you ghazals

David sang ten of his couplets out of the twenty-five that he had written. Of course we volleyed him with questions. I asked, 'Ghazals are something foreign to you, yet you have mastered the nuances beautifully, how did you manage this?' He said that the form had caught his attention through books on ghazals that he read in the US, and since then he has been working on it, steadily. In fact, he has been blogging on many forums and throws open his creations for feedback and criticism. He added, 'The idea is to stick to the form and yet find a way to express oneself through it, neither giving up the form nor one's expression, but endeavouring for a creation which synthesises both. It does seem difficult in the beginning but soon one finds his special corner wherein, even though he is in-the-box per say, the creation is still something out-of-the-box. Slowly and steadily, I learnt the principle of cadence, of using the most appropriate expression, of looking out for words which were neater and more compact. I became a student, trying to learn whatever I could from every suggestion that came my way, always testing it over and over again for flow, expression and rhythm. Very soon the form became me.'

What struck me was the effort that must have gone into mastering a form of poetry so alien to his milieu. His rendition was, of course, outstanding and showed his deep understanding and appreciation of this vocal form of poetry. Ghazals have to be recited in a very specific way. His immersion was complete. And this served to enhance the effect of the recital.

What I saw in David was pure love for the subject, unencumbered by expectations of money, fame, recognition. What guided his interest was his curiosity of the form and the longing to reach its depths.

Most of us had simply rushed through our readings, conscious of the audience, uncertain of our creations. For him, during his recital, nothing and no one existed; the world during those few minutes, not just for him but us as well, was just the ghazal that was being presented. Yes, through him we all experienced trance. I wondered when was the last time I myself had approached a subject with such perseverance, thoroughness and integrity.

Somewhere in the rigmarole of working within deadlines, achieving targets, following rules, being diplomatic, creating a balance, I had truncated my learning, ignored calls of a deeper understanding and compromised on my passion, as I did just enough to keep the momentum going. Yes, perhaps I have extracted the maximum out of myself, yet have done so purely from what other's want out of me. I have forgotten the pleasure that comes from learning or doing things for its own joy. Interestingly, I had not even realised what I was missing, until I saw what David had!

Yes, life is good and I am enjoying my work, but after meeting David, I felt that life can be still more beautiful, meaningful and perhaps more in tune with my within!

Raksha Bharadia

The Deal

I was very thin when I was in school and because of this, I could never defend myself. I was ragged a lot in school and later in BITS, Pilani too.

I remember Ramkumar Panhani; he was a back-bencher, while I sat in the third row. Every time he walked past me, he would hit me on the back of my head, just for fun! I would hurt and cry inside, but put up a brave face and sometimes even smile and try to shrug off the incident. At night in the dorm, I would wonder how long this would go on.

When I finished school and went to BITS, Pilani, I found that ragging in the school had been nothing! But, despite the fact that it was severe, I found the ragging in college to be essentially harmless. We had to clean our seniors' rooms and do things like wear my uncle's pink pyjamas!

I remember having this inferiority complex, though. I hadn't started shaving yet (I was all of sixteen years and four months when I started college). And so in a bid to look manly, I thought of trying out smoking. I procured some cigarettes and smoked one; it was Wills, I think. Immediately after my first puff, I felt giddy and fell down on my bed. I remember feeling even worse that I could not succeed at something as simple as smoking.

I vowed that I would continue trying till I could blow smoke rings like I had seen many a hero do in our Bollywood flicks. And I did it, in a month's time. I could smoke and I could blow smoke rings. I looked stylish with a fag, or so I thought! I loved getting photographed with a cigarette between my fingers; I was the master, the cigarette was my slave. Victory!

But reality was different. I was the slave and the cigarette, my master. Even though I tried, I could not stop. My lungs got affected, my health started deteriorating. I tried to stop several times, several hundred times, during my engineering days, then when I did my MBA and then when I began working. I could not.

I did score temporary victories: some lasted a week, a few almost a month, a couple of times I could refrain from smoking for six months at a stretch. But then I would go back, my resolve crumbled, my esteem a little wee lower. I would berate myself, tried self-hypnosis, but absolutely nothing worked. A whiff of smoke from someone smoking nearby, or even far away, would gently curl and enter my nostrils and, like an addict, I would submit to its command and light a cigarette.

I smoked for twenty-eight years of my life—how many cigarettes? How many rupees? At what cost to my lungs?

In 2000, I went for the Kailash Mansarovar yatra (why, I still do not know, for I am not the religious kind, nor did I believe in Shiva or any other god then). Before my departure, I remember that I was sitting in the Louis Kahn Plaza lawns of IIM-A (where I teach) near the steps, after my last class for that year. I smoked my last cigarette and made a 'deal' with Lord Shiva. I said to Him that I would not smoke for the entire yatra of thirty days, from the day I departed to the day I returned. That was my responsibility. But once I returned, the responsibility became His. Since He is the 'infinite', wasn't it only fair that he shouldered the larger burden between us? I almost heard Him say, 'It's a deal!'

It has been nine years now, and I haven't smoked a cigarette.

I kept my part of the bargain, and He has kept His part of the bargain.

Sunil Handa

My Little Step

One nice thing about the location of my flat is that it is a two-minute walking distance from a MORE grocery store. I generally go to MORE from home, so I take bags with me; if what I'm buying is small enough, I just put it in my purse (the size of which I actually chose for this purpose).

When you go to MORE, like any other grocery store, the cashier or his assistants automatically start to put things in a plastic bag. The first few times I got strange looks and had to repeat myself when I asked that they not put my groceries in plastic bags (and I don't think that was because they didn't understand my Gujarati accent). Over the course of a couple trips, I kept getting the same cashier, who asked me for the third time as he rang up my bill why I didn't take their bags. I quickly explained how plastic bags are bad for the environment, cause cancer and the deaths of cows. When I was about to leave, he stopped me and asked, 'Ma'am, can you fill out our comment form?'

I looked at the form, about to tell him that I needed to leave, when he interjected my thoughts with, 'I think you should share why you didn't want to take a plastic carrying bag.'

I looked at the form and again my mind told me that there was no point. But I quickly filled out the form, stating that

MORE should either stop providing plastic bags or encourage customers to bring their own bag (by potentially providing a financial incentive like stores in North America do), as that will show that the company cares about the environment, which is good for the company's image (I had to pitch it in corporate terms).

After that day, whenever the cashier rang up by bill, he never gave me a plastic bag. I was happy that at least my small action had made one other person learn about the dangers of plastic bags.

A bigger surprise came a month or two later. I walked into MORE after a long time and noticed a new sign on their announcement board behind the cashier and near the vegetables. It read: PLEASE MINIMISE THE USE OF PLASTIC BAGS.

MORE had not stopped giving plastic bags, but it at least had taken one step in the right direction.

Who said that you can't be the change?

Heena Patel

One Life

Our car, which was zooming up the Jamshedpur–Kolkata highway, slowed down. Ahead lay two men, injured and bleeding, surrounded by a crowd of people, simply staring.

Someone darted out of the crowd towards us. 'Please sir, help us. My friends are bleeding profusely. Please take them to the hospital.'

Without a moment of thought, a response was immediately given. 'We have no place to accommodate them,' the person driving said, shifting gears to speed away.

'But Pa, we could have easily adjusted. They needed help badly,' I said, from the backseat.

'Dimple don't act like a child. Where do you think we could have made place for the two of them?'

'Fine, perhaps not both, but at least one of them would have fit, Pa.' This came from my younger brother, Umang.

For my father, this was too much to bear. How could we kids question his judgement? Our audacity knocked hard against his towering walls of ego.

'You kids simply don't understand the consequences of getting involved in an accident. The work doesn't end with helping people to the doors of a hospital. I would have been running around police stations for the next couple of months and wasting my resources. I have no intentions of involving my name with the police. The others could have also helped. Why us?'

'But Pa it is—'

'—Dimple, now keep quiet. Don't argue with your father,' my mother interrupted.

Through the day, my thoughts lingered with those two men. I wondered what had happened to them. I prayed and hoped that someone who didn't have my father's ideology had helped them. My teenage spirit rebelled, and it was hard to accept that it was my father who had ended up not helping them. What did helping a dying man get to hospital have to do with the cops?

The next morning, I scanned the newspaper for news of the injured men. There it was, in bold letters: 'Two killed in accident on NH–33'.

So they finally died, I kept thinking. What insincerity! They teach us moral lessons to do what is right! I could not talk to my father. Perhaps somewhere deep inside, I held him responsible for those deaths.

Time passed and the memory of the accident faded. My mind was occupied with the many things that were going on, one of which was raksha-bandhan. I was specially looking forward to the festival. On August 3, two days before raksha-bandhan, Umang stayed back in school for basketball practice. An hour after he was supposed to have returned there was no sign of him and we began to get worried. All calls to the school elicited only this response: 'All players left the premises at 4.30 p.m. We have confirmed with the coach. Sorry, we have no further information'.

I went quickly to inform Mr Kapoor, our neighbour, and he, Pa and I immediately set out to look for Umang. Just near the school crossing, we saw a crowd. Yes, it was another accident. Pa did not pay much regard to the crowd and made to resume the search until some intuition made him turn back. Pa and I went through the crowd and came to a stunned halt. There, lying on the road, was a young boy. The uniform—a brown pant and white shirt—told us it was somebody from the same school as Umang's. Pa bent to take a closer look and was shocked into immobility. I had turned my head away, but then slowly turned towards the boy again, all the time thinking, 'Please, please I hope it is not Umang.' The final look scattered my prayers and I stood staring at my own younger brother.

Mr Kapoor lifted Umang in his arms and we drove to the nearest hospital.

Half an hour later the doctor appeared with the news that Umang had succumbed to his wounds. 'Had he been brought in time perhaps we could have saved him,' the doctor said.

I was shocked—my only brother had been snatched from me. I was filled with anger. I wanted to scream and shout, 'Umang died, Pa, because people did to him what you did to somebody. He died because people shrugged off a responsibility onto someone else's shoulders. He died because the world does not have a minute to spare for humanity.'

The tragedy has completely changed my father. Despite the rush or the hour, he always stops to help someone in need. It took Umang's death to finally make him realise the value of a human life. He now realises that even one life—whose ever it is—is precious.

This change taught me as well, and I took it as my responsibility to help Pa remain strong in his resolve to change as I no longer held any grudges against him. It was a new start and I am proud to call him my father.

Dimple Ranpara

The Dignity of Labour

It was five in the morning. The room smelt strange. I saw him, next to me, deep in slumber. I went to the bathroom and saw the reason for the stench. He had had a few extra drinks the previous night, must have thrown up all over the wash basin. The basin was clogged and the stink inside was unbearable. A little angry, I returned to the room with half a mind to wake him up and ask him to clean up. I could hear his soft snores and knew that he needed to sleep to be normal the next morning.

This happened when we were vacationing in Dubai during the Diwali holidays. I called up the reception and in an embarrassed tone explained my problem. It was a five-star property and the receptionist promised to send someone over within a minute. Before hanging up, I requested him to send a person with a pump to clear the basin out.

I went and sat on the bed, dreading facing the person who would be cleaning my husband's vomit at five in the morning.

He rang the bell. Asian surely—looked Indian, could have been a Bangladeshi. His curt 'Good morning' settled my doubts; he was surely from India, perhaps a Keralite. I gestured towards the bathroom door. All he said in his perfect English was, 'Just give me a few minutes ma'am.' Since I did not see him carrying any tool to clear the blockage

I said, 'Do you want to go and fetch a pump to clear the mess?' He answered, as politely, 'I have done this before ma'am, a pump is not what is required.'

I went and sat on the bed and waited for him to clean up. I could hear him, through the closed door. He emptied out the dustbin, took the plastic cover off and used the bin to drain out the filth from the basin with his hands. After which he cleaned the bin, stuffed the plastic in again, perhaps washed his hands and then opened the bathroom door.

He said, 'It is done ma'am. Perhaps you should ring up housekeeping to send someone with a room freshener.'

I asked him to wait, made the call to housekeeping and came back to him, extending a 100-Diram note (which is about 1,100 rupees in our currency). I said, 'I am sorry.'

He said, 'Ma'am I do this at least ten times a month. It does not hurt so much now.' I requested him to wait till the housekeeping man arrived. Many questions circled my mind. Why did he opt for such an unpleasant job, is money everything? Surely decent jobs were available in India too. Besides, I felt that I still needed to do something more to make up for what I'd made him do.

We chatted for about fifteen minutes and those minutes will be etched in my mind forever. R. Ramesh was indeed from Kerala. He had been in Dubai for the past eighteen years, before which he was in Kuwait on a similar job. He worked the night shift as a janitor for six days a week, eleven months a year. The twelfth month was what kept him going for the entire year. It was his official paid leave, which he spent in his small village with his wife, children and parents. Night shifts earned him more money, about thirty percent more, though there was more mess to be cleaned up like this.

I asked him, 'Why do you do this and that too so far away from your people, family . . .?'

He replied with as much dignity, 'My son just got admission

in an engineering college and my daughter passed her tenth Boards with a distinction. I can provide my mother with her daily medicines as she suffers from severe arthritis and my father, who has cleaned toilets all his life, can finally sit back and enjoy his cup of strong south Indian coffee with a newspaper. My job here in Dubai, amidst people alien to me, means my son will not be forced to do this for a living. He will be an engineer in a respectable company. My daughter, who wants to be a doctor, will at least not be required to suppress her ambitions because of a lack of funds. Tell me ma'am, can you think of one reason why I should not do this job? Besides, you cared enough to ask me about myself. I have already forgotten what I did and remember only a fellow Indian who showed empathy.'

I shook my head and thanked him for teaching me my most valuable lesson at five in the morning—so far away from my country, yet with my people!

Anonymous

The Finger Bowl

It had been a thoroughly enjoyable evening at the Sheraton. We were celebrating our son's entry into the world of wage-earners and had just finished dinner, when my mother-in-law did something that shocked us into realising that everything was not quite alright with her. She picked up the finger bowl and began to drink from it. She looked surprised, even gently puzzled, at the consternation and horror that erupted around that table. That one act made us take serious note of what everyone had till then, with amusement or irritation, accepted as behavioural lapses.

Tall, slim and attractive in her youth, my mother-in-law had grown only more elegant and gracious as she grew older. Always willing to help out and constantly keeping busy, she ran a tight ship and lived in her own house when she was not visiting her children.

Life had not exactly been a bed of roses for this gentle lady while her children were growing up. An absent husband in the line of duty and erratic pay cheques made her adept at stretching the last rupee and making it go a long way. And she managed it with dignity and humility. It couldn't have been easy, despite help from cousins, putting each of the children of five boys and two girls through school and professional college. Yet she managed.

When her husband retired, they finally set up a permanent home together. And in the evening of their lives, life changed for my mother-in-law in small ways. She could fly anywhere thanks to her pilot son, and money was no longer such an issue. But she continued to be her thrifty self and was as always loathe to ask anyone for anything, her children included. One boy she lost. In an air crash. He who had been part of the cabin crew. She was as always unafraid to meet adversity or disappointment with quiet but unbending determination.

Going to Canada alone to visit her Canadian daughter-in-law's family on her first-ever visit to anywhere, she was stranded at Heathrow due to a flash-strike. Everything was at sixes and sevens, but she somehow convinced the airlines to look after her till the strike ended, while others were made to fend for themselves. It was this quiet, steely resolve that was the hallmark of her character. She did everything with so much grace and dignity that even when people were unable to do what she thought she wanted, they would still go out of their way to help her.

After her husband died, she refused to move in with her children, preferring to visit them in turns or have them visit her whenever possible. Her house was where the action was. At any given point of time she had friends, family, and extended family drop in to hear proud stories of what her children were up to and enjoy the delicacies she still constantly churned out.

Thus it was from her nieces that we first heard about her now newly-acquired habit of repetition. None of us took it seriously. Or maybe we didn't want to .She was still travelling the world alone and was managing very well, or so we believed. Except for looking amused and rather exasperatedly telling her not to repeat herself so often, everyone went about his/her own busy, selfish business.

It took us a long time to realise that she was indeed very ill. And that all illnesses do not always necessarily manifest themselves physically. On an outing, once, she began picking up Pepsi caps from the street because they were shiny and pretty. With each such episode we would in embarrassment resort to impatiently chiding her or sharply taking her to task. Not for a moment did we stop to ponder the reason behind her behaviour.

In another instance we found her opening the front door late at night. Following her silently, wondering what she was up to, we found that she was totally lost—in every sense of the word. She seemed not to know where she was or who we were. But within seconds she appeared to be her normal self and told us quite charmingly that she was looking for her mother. On another occasion we found her prone on the floor; she didn't seem to know how she got there. The innocuous but incomprehensible incident of the finger bowl was to follow. And it set in motion a realisation, the repercussions of which impacted our lives instantly and immediately, for ever.

Tests followed. We were told that it was Alzheimer's and that there was no cure. She was put on Exelon. The signs had been there for us to see but all her clever children and their families had not realised it nor tried to find out why their normally clued-in mother was behaving so.

We had put it down to old age. Or perhaps again it was a state of denial, a sense of betrayal. Hard to tell. It was maybe easy to pretend that they were normal lapses and thus explainable. In our defence, all I can say is that we simply did not know it was a disease at all. It was also something that none of us knew how to comprehend, let alone handle or even realise that we were in it for the long haul.

On good days she remembered who we were. On other days she lived in the past—constantly looking for her mother, frenziedly packing and repacking a suitcase to go somewhere, or waiting for her school-going children. She would also, at times, revert to her youth. One particularly poignant episode was when she saw herself in the mirror and asked us who it was. When told, she argued it was not and then asked for her lipstick and eyeliner—to look better.

Sadly, other than her mind, there was really nothing at all wrong with her. There were times when we debated endlessly on which was worse, a physical or a mental illness. The latter wins hands down any day.

She grew more cunning each day, adept at hiding things from us or running out through the front door. Luckily for us, everyone knew her and of her condition and would bring her back. We began chaining the gate, locking the doors and hiding the keys. Her loss of dignity was complete. And that, more than anything else, is what is so awful about this dreadful disease.

My mother-in-law lived till she turned ninety last year. Gradually getting worse, with flashes of awareness becoming less frequent as the months went by. From the soft-spoken gentle soul she had been, she was now just the opposite. Also now prone to illogical tantrums, she was virulent in her anger and terrifyingly vocal. She was in turns childlike or frighteningly abusive. She was no longer the person we had known and life became difficult for all of us. We were told these were all classic symptoms of this uncompromising disease. She was apparently happy in her own world. It was we who had to learn how to cope. And we were not coping too well. We hired a trained permanent companion to live with her and visited her in turns. There was very little else we could do.

Though we've been told that we couldn't have done anything differently, more than a touch of regret remains. We were slow to realise that it was Alzheimer's and that it was a disease, yes, like no other, but a disease all the same. An abnormal behavioural disease brought on by physiological changes in the brain. It was not an embarrassment. Nor a lack of manners or a lack in comportment.

It needed to be handled differently, yes, but treated medically as well. With compassion and patience, with medicine and care. And above all it was the family and not the patient who needed to be counselled into coping. And that is perhaps where we fell short! The finger bowl is today a constant reminder.

Sreelata Menon

The King of Kings

It was fifteen days before Diwali and I was sorting through the cupboards. Every Diwali, I curse myself for accumulating so much throughout the year. Here were saris that I had not used since my marriage. I sighed and thought that perhaps I would need them again for some family occasion and I put them back inside.

Here were the children's storybooks that they were too old to read now. I rationalised that I would read them out to my grandchildren and back into the cupboard they went.

The number of things that we had in the house was incredible. There was a little glass violin that I didn't even know I had and I knew even less what I was going to do with. There were tiffin boxes old and new, there were badminton nets and racquets that the kids no longer played with. There were thousands of CDs that had to be sorted. There were mattresses and quilts that were falling apart from disuse.

In the end, I did what I inevitably do every time: I just put it all away neatly in the cupboard. Out of sight is out of mind! After all, I had better things to do. I had to pack for our family trip to Egypt.

'King of Kings am I, if anyone would know how great I am and where I lie, let him surpass one of my works.' Thus goes an inscription on an Egyptian sculpture. Our trip to Egypt helped me understand the meaning of these words and realise the greatness of Egyptian civilisation. One of our inevitable stops was the pyramids, one of the Seven Wonders of the Ancient World.

Along with the mummies of the pharaohs, we saw buried the artefacts used throughout the king's life. These artefacts ranged from decorated chests, to gold bracelets and necklaces, to alabaster vases and caskets, to combs and cosmetics. There were girdles and games, there were chairs and mirrors and sandals. These were the people who had lived so luxuriously. These were the most powerful people on the planet. Even today, the power that an ancient Egyptian pharaoh had can seem unbelievable. And yet, here they were, in their glass coffins, without any vestment of their former glory, being gawked at by awe-struck tourists.

I couldn't help laugh at their foolishness in believing that they could enjoy luxuries even after their death. I wondered at the amount of trouble they took to preserve their belongings. And where is that glorious kingdom they built? To quote Shelley:

Nothing beside remains. Round the decay
Of that colossal wreck, boundless and bare,
The lone and level sands stretch far away.

Nothing is permanent, I realised, looking at the mummies of the kings.

And then it struck me—that is what I do too, give such importance to maintaining my possessions. Every morning, I go through the house, checking if every speck of dust has been removed. Now, my daughter tells me, 'Loosen up mum, after a hundred years it's not going to matter at all if your house was a little imperfect.'

It's hard for me to give up a habit ingrained over the years, but I'm determined to try. I have understood that I spend too much time accumulating objects for my house, and then I spend an equal amount of energy maintaining them.

What really counts is the time spent together with our dear ones doing the things that we enjoy. These days, I shut my eyes and think of the things that really give me happiness. It's opening the door in the morning and seeing the carpet of parijaat flowers in my garden. It's sitting out in the garden during the rain and just smelling the earth. It's laughing at my dog's goofiness. Things we own don't really matter; it's our varied experiences that give us happiness!

Bhagyashree Sowani

The Principles of Justice and Humanity

My father-in-law, the Hon'ble Justice M.P. Thakkar, didn't like me using the 'official' car for personal reasons.

Born in Myanmar, with a silver spoon in his mouth, Justice Thakkar once had a thriving practice as a lawyer, but an underlying urge to serve society prompted him to leave it and join the judicial services at a rather measly pay, overlooking the fact that he had a large family consisting of nine children, aged parents and one sister. He had always been moved by the suffering of the poor and needy, and firmly believed that humanity should be man's highest credo. A man of principles, ethics and morals, he never swerved from them and strived to make his family members tread the same path.

And so, on that day, despite my panic and the ticking of the clock, he was adamant on not allowing me to use the official vehicle. I finally managed to reach the airport on time, in another car of course, but his stringent attitude had upset me.

When I reached the airport, I met Justice S.H. Sheth, a friend of my father-in-law's, who had retired from the judiciary and had started practising in the Supreme Court. I paid him my respects and we started talking. He suddenly became very emotional and started narrating an incident.

'Last week I was representing a client in the court of a two-judge bench, comprising Justice Thakkar and another judge. My client was the tenant of a widow. My client had not paid the rent for a year and that is why the landlady had filed the particular case for recovery of rent.

'Justice Thakkar was inclined towards the tenant while the other was pro landlord. Everybody in the court was waiting for the judgement. According to the Rent Act, the tenant was bound to pay the rent on that particular day itself. The total outstanding rent was Rs 10,000.' (This was a hefty amount at the time this incident took place—equivalent to a month's salary of a Supreme Court judge.)

'When the judgement was delivered, it favoured the landlady and the tenant was ordered to pay the complete amount, that very day. I was particularly upset with the judgement, as I was sure that Justice Thakkar would consider the difficulty of the tenant. By evening that day, I and my client were almost in tears, worried about how he would pay the rent.

'Just as we were discussing the distressing situation, the doorbell rang. A peon from Justice Thakkar had come to the office with an envelope, which he handed over to me. Enclosed was a cheque of Rs 10,000 along with a note that read: *When I am presiding as a judge, I have to abide by the duties of a judge, but I cannot forget that I am also a human being, and I cannot overlook the pathetic condition of another fellow human. Please accept the cheque.*'

This incident added to my already long list of reasons as to why my father-in-law was such a respected and admired man—including his refusal to let me use the official car for personal reasons.

Vrunda Thakkar

True Greatness

It was one of those breakfast talks that are often organised by groups of businessmen. Normally, I would have only heard about them if I had happened to read the business section of the newspaper the day after the event, but in this case, the keynote speaker happened to be one of the major supporters of the non-profit that I work for, so my presence was required.

Finding information on him was surprisingly easy, and I had read up as much as I could on him before the conference. Wikipedia informed me that he is the chairman of a power company that supplies more than seventy-five per cent of Hong Kong's power requirements, and of a company that owns hotels that have been voted as some of the best in the world. That he's been awarded knighthood by Queen Elizabeth II, and been made an officer of the Legion of Honour by the government of France. I found out that he was a fixture on the Forbes list of the world's two hundred richest men, and that the foundation that carries his family name gives away huge sums of money to charity. Though I knew all there was to know about him, I hadn't been able to find a picture of his, so had no idea what he looked like.

I was networking furiously before the talk—when you work for a non-profit, you learn to approach everyone you meet like a potential funder, and launch into your spiel before their attention starts waning. Seeing this well-dressed gentleman next to me, I introduced myself to him and handed him my business card. When he told me his name, I was momentarily taken aback—he was the keynote speaker. Before I could recover my poise, he was whisked away. To be honest, I was more than happy to have just been able to shake his hand.

Two hours later, after the talk was over, I was standing near the exit, waiting for my boss to say her good-byes. I noticed the keynote speaker making for the exit—he had shaken all the hands he was required to shake, and was on the way out. He caught sight of me and walked across, 'I am sorry I cut our conversation short so abruptly,' he said. 'Pray, continue.'

I spent the next few minutes talking about my organisation and the work we did. And about the difference that his support and contribution was making to us. He was a patient listener, often interjecting a question or comment, but mostly just taking in what I had to say. He needn't have heard me out—I did not tell him a single thing that was not already mentioned in much greater detail in the reports we sent him. But he still heard me out, because he thought it was the right thing to do.

I finally understood the meaning of the word 'great'.

Is it any wonder the man is lauded more for his values than for his wealth.

Rayna Talwar

Working for People

All my life I have never worked for anyone except myself.
I have worked because I wanted to—keeping the balance between family and work. Have never ever shirked housework because it was 'my' home and also have never been without work because somehow work seems to find me. Even during the ten years of 'maternity leave' that I took, I produced a newsletter for the community that I lived in, ran a library and produced a play! Besides, there is always a home that demands 24 x 7 attention.

I never started off with fat salaries. When I began my job at Raymonds, I started on a salary of Rs 350 and when I left I reached just Rs 1,200.

Ten years later at Blue Star, I did reach figures of three and four thousand, but soon had to go back to Rs 1,200 when I started my teaching career. From then on, it has been a gradual rise till I reached Rs 10,000. In the course of this, I have worked with heads that were adamant on not giving me the rise that was my due till providence compelled them, took the matter out of their hands and at one stroke tripled my pay packet.

I have never worked *for* a position or a designation at any time because I never had a high position! I was always surrounded by people who felt I could do something for them and I simply did it. And for all of them, I was simply Lakshmi. Later I did get a very big title—teacher. What is the role of the teacher? The same as that of a parent: bring up children, teach them values, teach them to attain their potential. This is the one designation I have cherished and valued the most and just continued with it—only the size and age of the people I taught changed.

I have never worked for organisations or people—yet I have been very devoted and sincere in my work in every place I worked. At the end of the day I have moved out gracefully, with mixed feelings—joy in the warmth and emotion with which people said farewell to me, and sorrow because I had to leave. I've also gone back to them when I could and enjoyed the pride they feel in my growth.

I remember my first boss who literally brought me up from a callow eighteen-year-old to a mature twenty-seven-year-old—a stern taskmaster who would not let a spelling mistake or a comma be out of place. Yet he took as much care of me as my father—paid for my college education, ensured that I was escorted home when I worked late, added tremendously to my reading, visited my homes wherever I lived and ensured that I was happy.

I have worked for the students I taught—right from 1984 onwards. I still think of them. With the progress in today's means of communication, they come back after years to ask 'How are you?' and to say 'Don't give up teaching'.

I work for my husband—who from the time I have known him, took pride in my abilities and gave me the space to work, who never put a stumbling block in whatever I did. I work for the smile with which he sends me to work every morning (and the compliments he gets from the wives of his friends!). I work for the pride he takes in my small achievements and the unfailing encouragement to broaden my mind.

I work for my children—who helped me with my B.Ed and got me every teaching assignment. Only when they felt that our being in the same school was a hindrance to our progress, did I start working in a different school.

Today, when I stand and look at the fingers pointing at me because I seem to be working for two organisations, I wish I could tell them I am only doing what a teacher should do— teach the ones willing to learn from me. If I have been a good teacher and made a difference to some, I am working to extend that to many. Do I need to transfer paper or information from one organisation to another? Not at all, because in the words of a popular song—'I came empty-handed and will go away also empty-handed'. And still continue to work—doing what I can. I work *for* people that think I can work for them, not for organisations. I work for people that are happy to have me working with them and are neither threatened nor insecure of what I may do. I work for people that greet me with a smile, tell me what to do and at the end of the day let me go home in peace. I work for people that ask me to do something for them, benefit from it and simply say a 'thank you'. I work for people that accept me and my work.

I will always work for people that allow me to work for myself!

Lakshmi Madhusoodanan

4
A NEW LEASE

*L*ife is a process. We are a process. The universe is a process.

—Anne Wilson Schaef

A Messiah in Malaysia

Death visits us in different forms. Sometimes it holds your head down in the water and then, inexplicably, lets you go.

Kuantan, Malaysia, 1989.

As newlyweds, we were slumming it out on a beach resort. It wasn't the kind with a pool and French cuisine—instead, there were shacks on stilts with grass roofs and a mosquito net to keep the swarming bugs away at night. The front door opened to the whispering susurrations of the Straits of Malacca; the back door looked over an ancient Muslim cemetery with frugal headstones jutting out of fetid ground.

We went swimming with a local guide. Mohan was a large Tamilian, whose lumbering shape belied his ability to swim through the water as if he had fins. The seafood served at the hawker stall by the beach had traces of sand, but it washed down quite well with Tiger beer. We weren't at all bothered when the waiter told us that three teenagers had died on this beach two days ago, sucked into one of the whirlpools that lurked beneath the placid waters. It was a day of bright sun on blue waters reflecting a clear sky. We wallowed in the warm water to surface briefly for a cool drink or a spicy bite, then kept running back through the powdery sand into a gently heaving sea.

The evening sun had dipped lower in the horizon when the

waves came in, the tide slow at first, and then insistently pulling us away from the shore with every exhalation of the sea. By the end of the day, this rocking motion felt soporific, even as it pulled us far from shore. Suddenly, Mohan was a dark speck in the vast ocean as the beach retreated, very far away.

Panicked, my husband and I swam towards the shore, but the pull of the sea was inexorable. My husband, never a strong swimmer, started to tire. In the salt-water, it became easier to pull him up by his hair as his body grew increasingly limp. It is strange how the mind disengages—two months ago, a relative had died in a Delta air crash in Detroit, leaving behind a bride of six months, and I remember watching my husband fight the water and wondering how I would tell his family. Watching my husband struggle to the surface, I thought: how does any woman tell her in-laws that their son is dead?

There was no doubt in my mind that I would survive. That I would survive without him, already felt like an unbearable burden.

Then there was a speck of wet blond hair swimming towards us, and a man miraculously appeared by our side. Without asking whether we needed help, he towed us both to safer waters with powerful strokes. When he asked, Is there anyone else?, I could only point to Mohan, now a bobbing head in the horizon, and our saviour disappeared into the sea. We learnt later, after Mohan was found exhausted but still alive, and people had helped us to the local hospital, that our benefactor was a Hawaiian lifeguard vacationing in Kuantan. Although none of the people on the beach could hear our cries for help, he had read our body language from the distance of the beach and realised we were in distress.

We scoured the hotels in the area, but we only had a description created out of our terrified minds, not even a name, and we never found him.

It is twenty-one years since that day, yet I still marvel at how close the margins are between death and life. Each anniversary is sweeter because of our memory of that day in Kuantan; it is a memory which surfaces easily when a child dashes across a busy street or an old man starts to choke on a morsel in his throat. Never take love for granted.

But most of all, the incident in Kuantan taught me the value of this Malay pantun: *Hutang emas boleh di bayar, hutang budi di bawa mati*. Debts of gold can easily be repaid, but debts of gratitude are carried to the grave.

Some debts are indeed carried to the grave.

Dipika Mukherjee

A Second Chance

5 January 1989.

'There do you see that?' Ranbir asked.

'Where?' I said, tilting my head, more to be closer to him than to actually see the stars he was pointing to.

'Right there, that's the Orion, four stars on the outside and three in a line inside!'

Yeah, I could see it all right. But my heart wasn't beating that loud because of the stars. I was sixteen; it was the first time I'd ever stood so close to him. A strange concoction of emotions. Despite the racing pulse and the throbbing heart, there was serenity in the whole moment. A feeling of belonging ... of coming home.

4 February 2009.

'There can you see that?' I asked.

'No, where?' said my sweetheart, my darling daughter, all of ten.

'There, Sanya, the four stars make a square and the three inside are in a line,' I said, pointing up while giving my swing a push.

'Who told you about this con ... conselation?' she asked.

'Constellation! It's the Orion,' I corrected. 'My boyfriend told me a long, long time ago.'

'The one with the Dracula teeth?' she giggled.

'Badmash bachcha ... see if you can go higher than this,' I pushed my swing higher and both of us burst out laughing.

5 February 2009.

One new message on Facebook

Ranbir Sabharwal; 4 February at 9.41 p.m.

Hi, You are a tough one to find. Read all the reviews about your work. AWESOME. Wanna get in touch?

On a recent vacation to the US with my family, my brother had asked me if I ever bumped into Ranbir, my ex-boyfriend, or if I knew anything about him. I'd replied saying these kind of things happen only in the movies, not in real life! I guess that was the time when I finally allowed myself to think about him again. The recesses of my mind opened up just a wee bit, still careful not to let the light through. And slowly I had the courage to talk about my past, a part of my life that I had sliced off and pretended never existed.

And now, after thirteen years, this message on Facebook! My world was swirling!

Would it have been different if Ranbir and I had finally gotten married? If he hadn't made me wait seven years for a commitment? If I'd been a little more patient? If we hadn't had a fight? If he hadn't gone away to the ship? If we could have at least amicably said good-bye? Would it have been different if I hadn't subsequently met Sanya's father? If Sanya's father hadn't balmed my aching heart and taken me under his wing? Would it have been different if I'd been more conscious of our age difference and his seeming ineligibility due to a past failed marriage and three children?

I remember I was hurting and ready to take on the world for love. But then again, I had so much to learn. I wouldn't know so many things, had I not gone through whatever I did.

I wouldn't have known what freedom meant, until I'd borne the marks of that first strike from the one I thought would lead me to my salvation. I wouldn't have learnt how to bear till I thought I couldn't bear anymore, and then go ahead and learn to bear some more. I wouldn't have known the pain in love if I hadn't loved and lost. I wouldn't have learnt how to pick up the pieces. And I wouldn't have learnt that my soul is far from being battered.

If I hadn't gone through what I did, I wouldn't have learnt how to ultimately forgive Sanya's father for the public humiliation and the forced carnal pleasures. I wouldn't have known how to forgive him for the drunken brawls and the bruised skin. I wouldn't have learnt that the skin heals much faster than the scars on a heart; but most importantly, I wouldn't have learnt that the heart too does heal. I wouldn't have learnt to move on, and in moving on I wouldn't have found how life makes a turn around.

If I hadn't gone through whatever I did, I wouldn't have known the moment that would make me hold her in my arms, her very first touch, her cry, her gurgle. I wouldn't have known her first suckle on my body and the umbilical bond that she would form, with my soul, the moment the cord was cut from my womb.

I wouldn't have known how my heart would break when I would stand at the threshold of justice, facing a battery of lawyers, fighting against the embarrassment of riches that he holds and the strength that he shows in ripping the one joy I would clutch tight in my arms. In that moment I wouldn't have known the wail of a mother and the strength of my character to stand up and against all odds that were and will ever be. I wouldn't have known how to survive and I wouldn't have known what a winner I would be.

If I hadn't gone through whatever I did, I wouldn't have learnt to hold on and hang in there and fight the temptation to run away. I wouldn't have known the dark as I stared into the night, and I wouldn't have known that there would eventually be light. I wouldn't have known how to find faith within myself. And I wouldn't have learnt how to hold on to it. Though life may not have gotten easier with time, I wouldn't have known that the strife would nurture me fine.

It's been a few months since the message from Ranbir. I've since learned that he got married soon after our break-up and has a nine-year-old daughter, Sugandha, the apple of his eye. He is the captain of his ship now; though life hasn't been too kind to his relationship with his wife—they are divorced. We both seemed to have paid a heavy price for letting go of what we had. He is coming home later this year. And I am hoping for life to give me a second chance. A chance to say good-bye and finally move on. . . .

Suparnaa Chadda

A Second Innings

Browsing in a bookstore in Lucknow, a friend came across a book titled *Marwadih ka Masheea*. Marwadih is the name of the place where we stay in Banaras. My friend casually flicked through it and discovered that the book was about my father and how hard he had worked for the people in Marwadih to give them a better life. When my friend discovered this book, my father had already been dead for more than five years. He had passed away at the age of sixty, to cancer.

And yet, at the age of thirty-seven, my father knew he was dying. Sometimes you can feel death around you, and he felt death around him constantly. He had been unwell for a long time and was just getting weaker.

He had started hiccupping all the time; sometimes violently, sometimes softly. His hiccups would not stop, even when sleeping, and whatever he ate he would vomit if there was a violent hiccup. And the accompanying fever, though low, was persistent. Despite conducting various tests, the doctors could not find a reason behind his strange ailment.

Thirty-seven was such a young age. Two of his children were barely reaching their teens whilst his youngest was yet a toddler. A totally self-made man, he had worked hard to make his business a success. Living frugally, he built an enviable house, one that he was fiercely proud of.

He was put into the ICU with various tubes and pipes running in and out of his body. My mother was always by his side, sobbing quietly, constantly. The doctor came in with the latest set of test results. He was perplexed as all the results were mostly clear. He was just constantly hiccupping and unable to swallow anything. No medication of any kind had any effect.

He was slowly deteriorating. He was on the drip and classified as a serious case.

My father had always been a great devotee of Hanumanji. On that particular evening, my father felt someone near his bed. There was a rustle and he saw a shadow. He knew, he was absolutely, positively, sure, that it was Hanumanji.

'Has my time come?' he asked Him.

'Yes,' He said.

'Please,' my father said, 'my children are small, give me another twenty-five years.'

My father says he felt a hand on his head and then he heard a whisper, 'Your wish shall be granted.'

The next thing he knew, my father saw his doctor standing near him. He looked around the room. There was no one else. Had it been a dream?

'Your fever has finally gone down. And after a long time you have finally had a peaceful sleep.'

His hiccups started decreasing soon after, and a week later he was discharged from the hospital. He had been declared totally fit.

My father used to say that his second lease of life was thanks to Hanumanji.

My father prospered but he never forgot that he was living on borrowed time. If God had given him another chance, he knew that he had to do something to be worthy of it and to make Him proud. My father involved himself whole-heartedly in charity work. We lived in a place totally dominated by caste demarcations, and he worked towards breaking those barriers.

He wanted to do more ... but what?

Education! More than anything else, my father believed that education was one of the cornerstones of a strong society. And so, he opened a school for underprivileged children.

And he went to Sanket Mochan every day to thank Hanumanji for His benevolence and blessings.

And that is how my father lived the rest of his life. One morning, when he was sixty—his responsibilities over, my siblings and I married and well settled—he got up, feeling unwell. He had started hiccupping again—and he knew that his time was up.

He went to the doctor. Test results showed that he had advanced liver cancer, and very little time.

My father died after a year. He prayed all the time to Hanumanji. He embraced death with happiness. At his funeral there were about a hundred children. They were the children from the school that he had started. There were so many, many people whom we did not know; people whom he had helped during their times of crisis.

My dad had six cows, which he regularly fed fresh fruits to at least once a day. When his body was taken out of the house, they all mooed together loudly, as if in farewell and tribute to my father.

Not a single eye was dry amidst the large gathering of friends, relatives and well-wishers.

I miss my father very much, but very rarely do I dream of him. However, the few times that I have, the dream has always been the same: it is a Saturday, and he is immersed in Sanket Mochan, doing seva for his Hanumanji, the God he loved and trusted so much.

And if anything, I know that that is where my father's spirit rests today—with his beloved Hanumanji.

Anu Chopra

Fine Line

X.J. Kennedy's poem *Seven Deadly Virtues* makes you think about the fine line between vice and virtue. What he says of good cheer is rather disturbing for anyone who has been through periods of despondency:

Good Cheer

When grief and gloom are what you want, good cheer is nothing but a big pain in the rear.

I have known the effort it takes to get excited about the beautiful weather outside, leave the familiar confines of the well-worn couch to make the best of what the day has to offer. I don't know that I have wanted 'grief and gloom' at times like this, but have lacked what it takes to bring 'good cheer' on spontaneously.

The craving for uninterrupted quietness and to be left alone was far more than any desire to seize the day. I suffered knowing that my mood would permeate J's, diminishing her natural joie de vivre, that I would feel guilty long after for it. I would want to undo that day, that hour, have made some happy memories with my child.

But when the neighbour's kid knocked on the door to ask, 'Mommy wants to know if you and J would like to come watch my soccer game', something inside snapped as if the strands of gloom were ripped apart by an unexpected burst of happiness—the smiling face of a little girl who wanted me to become part of her day.

Heartcrossings

One Rainy Day in Mumbai

From my window in office, I looked up at the dark clouds hovering threateningly, wondering if this would be the day the city was waiting for. Then, brushing drenched images aside, I added a slide to my presentation—with lots of boxes and arrows. Things that my work life was now surrounded by. I stepped out into the dark a full two hours later, carrying a small backpack and a heavy package that I'd received from my parents.

Bandstand is usually a lovely place. Most days I step out of office to the beautiful shades of sunset over the sea, trying to hold my own against the strong wind. It's crowded with huddled couples, eager rickshaws and an occasional movie unit. Well, today was not exactly the same. I squinted to spot a run-down Premier Padmini amidst the drizzle, crossing the road twice to try my luck on both sides. No one wanted to make the trip.

Finally I flagged down an auto-rickshaw and hurried into it, cardboard box and all, asking him to take me to the farthest point into the city to which he was allowed. We passed by the seaface, the radio blaring *Barso re megha megha*. I hummed along, the sea breeze blowing the shorter strands of my hair all over my face. My super-dramatic alter ego was busy, fancying myself as a pretty heroine under a gorgeous waterfall, splashing around and getting drenched without a second thought. I put my hand outside the rickshaw to catch the raindrops—what any self-respecting actress would do. And then suddenly the movie stopped, like a power-cut in a village talkie.

'Yahan se taxi le lena madam.'—*Take a taxi from here.*

A different final point for the autos. I took my own time paying him, hoping a cab would stop by us. No such luck. Getting down gingerly, I focused on the road, hoping to see a cab coming my way. Nothing. I surveyed the surroundings. Dark and empty, the drizzle was slowly morphing into a full-blown downpour. Several empty autos. One stationary cab filled with four men. A lonely lady with wares of potato wafers and two Bisleri bottles under a small umbrella. This is Mumbai, I thought, it's always safe. Finally a taxi. Damn. People in it. Several minutes passed on the empty road. No luck. The rain was falling heavily by now and I could feel the droplets running down my neck.

'Goa ja rahe ho?'—*Going to Goa?*

I turned around sharply to see the Bisleri woman standing next to me with her little umbrella.

'Mahim,' I said, managing a wry smile.

'Taxi chahiye?'—*Want a taxi?*

I nodded, trying to decipher any hidden messages in her words. Things I usually don't pick up.

She came closer to me and held the umbrella over my head and yelled out a name. Four kids came running out of nowhere like pixies from an Enid Blyton novel. They rushed off in different directions on receiving orders from the woman. One older boy stayed behind.

'Soch raha tha kiske liye chhaata pakadke khadi ho,' he told her.—*I was wondering who you were holding the umbrella for.*

She replied, 'Bacchi akeli khadi thi na.'—*The girl was standing alone, you know.* 'Meri bhi do bacchi hai, tum jaisi,'—*I have two daughters just like you*, she smiled.

I smiled at her wondering what I should say. Was this a trap? Why would she do this?

'Mein pakad lun?' *Shall I hold the umbrella?* I asked, although my hands were full with my things. Frankly, amidst the hundred thoughts that were running through my mind, none of them involved holding her umbrella. Yet I heard myself saying it.

I never heard her reply. It was muffled by shouts of 'Aunty' and 'Didi' that suddenly rung the air. The little kids ran towards us, followed by a taxi which truly seemed to have appeared out of thin air. Before I could react they shuffled me in, their grimy wet faces smiling at me from the different windows. From the one I sat at, I could now see her wares, cold and unprotected in the rain.

Stunned, I mumbled a 'thank you' under my breath and waved at the five excited children and the Bisleri woman. They waved till I went out of sight.

I reached home safely that night. Drenched, but safe. And with the wonderful feeling that comes when a total stranger makes you smile.

Sandhya Krishnan

Requiem for Love

Mrinal and I were close friends in school. I hadn't met him since I got married and so was delighted when he called up to tell me that a business meeting had brought him to the station where I was posted. He was the only one in our batch who remained a bachelor whilst the rest of us from the class of '66 had wed in the '70s, a good two decades before this incident. When I came home that evening, I told my wife that we were having a guest for dinner the next day.

'What's his name,' she asked.

'Mrinal,' I said. 'Mrinal Sen.'

'Is he coming with his wife?'

'No, he's single,' I replied. 'Though why he has chosen to remain in that state is something I've never understood.'

The next day he arrived on schedule and the next two hours flew by in happy reminiscences of times gone by.

Over dinner, my wife casually asked him why he had chosen to remain single. He was silent for a while and I tried to change the subject, sensing his discomfiture. 'It's all right,' he said, cutting me off. 'It's been so many years since anybody asked me that question, and truth to tell, I've never answered it yet. It started very innocently. She was the daughter of a business acquaintance of my father and we met at a party. She walked up to me and introduced herself. "I'm Sara. I believe our parents have similar business interests."

'Her voice was soft and gentle. I was mesmerised when I looked into her eyes, and in that instant I fell hopelessly in love for the first time in my life. That evening, I was embarrassingly tongue-tied and awkward and she must have passed me off as an idiot who could not even blabber.

'I found out that she was working in her father's firm and a few days later I went over to meet her. Well, that was the start of a long romance, for soon we were seeing each other rather frequently. I had no idea where the relationship was headed and was content to just be with her. Sometimes we had dinner out together, but for the most part it was talking over the phone or taking a walk in the park. And about six months later, I proposed to her.

'We were sitting in the park when I asked her to marry me. Her eyes lit up, but she did not answer me. Instead she posed a question. "Will your parents accept me?" she asked.

'"I haven't discussed it with them yet," I told her. I held her hand and squeezed it gently, but she was far from being reassured.

'"Your parents are wonderful people, but they struck me as very conservative. What will happen if they don't approve?" Her tone was soft but I could detect the anxiety it portrayed.

'Still holding her hands, I looked into her eyes. "It's about the woman I love; of course they will accept you."

'She smiled weakly. "Let's wait till you speak with them," was all she said.

'She was more aware of the strength of societal pressures than I was. Or perhaps I had a misplaced faith in my capability to win my parents over. When I spoke to them that evening, that fact came painfully to light.

'"I have asked Sara to marry me." Seven simple words were all it took to shake the very edifice of peace in my family. My father froze as if in shock. Mom appeared paralysed. Then after what seemed an eternity, my father rose from his chair. He was seething with rage. When he walked away wordlessly to his room and shut the door behind him I knew I stood accused of letting him down.

'I looked to my mother for support but none was forthcoming. She said, "Sara is a wonderful girl, but she does not belong to our caste. You cannot disregard the customs of our people. And our religious beliefs are different too."

'Over the next two weeks, I tried to make my parents understand, but they refused to budge. During this entire period I didn't meet Sara, neither did I call her. I did not know how to handle the conflicting emotions raging within my heart. My father had withdrawn into a shell and my mother was totally listless. I was well and truly caught between my love for Sara and my duty to my parents. Finally, I sacrificed Sara on the altar of custom and tradition. I had to convey my decision to Sara personally. That was the least that honour demanded of me. When I met her, I could see the strain on her face. She must have anticipated the worst and my demeanour merely confirmed her fears. "I'm sorry Sara," was all I could say. There was no need to say anything else. My face said it all.

'She was silent for some time, and then she started crying. I could see the hurt in her eyes. I made my way painfully to the door and she walked behind me. I could have turned back, held her hand and married her the very same day, but I didn't ... Instead I walked out of her house and her life. In that brief moment I died a thousand deaths, and my soul died too.

'Now you know why I am still single,' Mrinal said, looking at us. 'I knew I had made the wrong decision and I could never forgive myself for it. From then on, I foiled each and every attempt of my parents to get me married. I had to bear my cross alone.'

'Don't be too hard on yourself,' my wife said. 'Societal pressures are not that easily cast off.'

'That may be true,' Mrinal replied. 'But I can't claim not to have been aware of what society expected of me. While I had made no promises to my parents, I had committed myself to Sara. And I broke that commitment. I wronged her. My parents were afraid of what people in our society would think of them and I was afraid of hurting my parents. In the final analysis, I let a faceless society set the agenda for my life and I lost what was most precious to me.'

Mrinal prepared to leave and we bade each other goodbye. But my wife surprised me with her next words.

'Mrinal—Sara *has* forgiven you ...'

Mrinal looked at her, uncomprehendingly.

'It's time to let go of the ghosts of the past,' she said. 'Sara and I were friends in college, and we've keep in touch. I know how hurt she was when you left her, but even then she could not bear to hear anything said against you. She forgave you many years ago and is happily married now. The past is over. It's time you forgave yourself.'

Dhruv Katoch

Science Versus Spirituality

India has produced some world-class doctors, and certainly, Dr Ashok Seth would be considered one of them. A top-of-the-line professional, he has been instrumental in introducing techniques like angiograms and angioplasties in the Asia Pacific region and has, on an average, performed almost forty such diagnostic and coronary intervention techniques on a daily basis. He is revered by the kith and kin of the patients whose lives he has helped save. But this is not why I write about him.

When we met, my attention was immediately drawn to the vibhuti he had applied on his forehead. 'I am a Satya Sai Baba devotee,' he explained. A doctor, trained to think rationally and logically, who believes in a higher power? 'Of course,' he said. 'What if I walk out of here today and the driver slams the door on my hand. Wouldn't that be the end of my career? My skill and ability to save lives is His grace.'

'But such unwavering faith . . . have you had an experience with God,' I probe further. He answers with an emphatic nod. 'Miracles do happen, and I am a living example of that.'

Apparently Dr Seth belongs to a family that has always been religious, but for him, faith was just a positive way of life, nothing more nothing less. Until eight years back when, inexplicably, the entire left side of his body was paralysed.

No amount of treatment yielded any results and he had resigned himself to perhaps never moving his arm again, let alone holding an instrument in his hand for any kind of an operation. As a last resort, it was decided that his spine would have to be operated upon. On the insistence of his wife and family, he went to Puttaparthi (Satya Sai Baba's ashram near Bangalore) to take Baba's blessings before he flew to the US for the procedure. 'With a letter in my hand in the large gathering of thousands of devotees waiting for a mere glimpse of Baba, my mind was as numb and motionless as the left side of my body,' he recalls. 'In that daze, I realised that Baba had finally come up to me. Without me saying a word, he stroked the left side of my body three times and walked away. The rest was a miracle.' By the evening of the same day, he remembers, the pain was slightly less for the first time in six weeks. Still sceptical, he did not mention it to his family. Within ten days, he vouches, the pain was gone and he was back to work. The spinal operation obviously never took place. Till date he continues to perform angioplasties and helps save more lives.

So while the argument about science and religion not being complementary to each other may continue, for me, science and spirituality have always been in alignment, but perhaps unless one experiences it, one will continue to be parochial about it.

Suparnaa Chadda

Someone

There in the crib lay a small, perfect baby. Brown eyes, black hair curling softly over the face, fist bunched over a pouty mouth. Three days old. What was it to me?

Not my child but so much my own. The busy hospital rushed around me. No one knew I had come, no one had told me that the infant was on the way. But I knew. Friends had whispered into my ears. Through malice, or maybe a desire to pass on information. I did not care; I was there to greet the child.

Endometriosis. Chocolate bubbles of blood simmering like evil soup in the inner recesses of my womb. Twelve years ago it had erupted into my life and the surgeon's knife had cut away all my dreams. Or so I had thought.

Dev and I were, as you would say, 'childhood sweethearts'. We had been there for each other for most of our lives and you would have thought that that was the way it would always be. You and all the others would be so wrong.

The surgeon told Dev that endometriosis could cause infertility. I might never be able to have a child.

Ten days after he escorted me tenderly back from the hospital, Dev told me that he was seeing someone else and that we had no future together. It could not have been plainer. No children meant no use for me.

Or, as he said so reasonably, it was not that I was in love with him. The moments of intimacy meant nothing. Just one of those things. Where did the silly word, that meaningless word called 'love' come in a relationship between two consenting adults? Nowhere.

I let him go. I hoped the 'love' would die, and all that seems unaccountably like pain with it. And buried them together with memories. Do you think that hearts break? Or is it that it mends and carries on? Or do you think it becomes warped forever?

And then, you know, when there is only debris around you, miracles are granted. Magic works. I met the cousin of an old friend at a family gathering. He asked me out and listlessly I agreed. Surprisingly, I enjoyed his company. He had this wonderful ability to make me laugh. One thing led to another and six months later he asked me to marry him.

I was aghast. 'But Akash . . . I have endometriosis . . . I will not be able to have children.' Someone must have laughed overhead because Akash held my hands very tightly and said, 'Listen, that means nothing. Sure, we both love children, but right now it is you and I who matter. Whatever you have, whatever it is . . . it means nothing.' And Someone smiled.

Reader, I married him. I married a man for whom endometriosis meant nothing. Who hummed the same old tunes that I had loved. Who in these short months had showed me that the sixteen years with Dev was an absolute zero in terms of faith and that much misused word, 'love'. A sweet and lovely man who steadied my life and my work as a counsellor. I had three wonderful children. Two daughters and a son. My family was my life. An anchor which nothing could change.

Dev married the girl for whom he had ditched me. Outwardly everything was perfect. But they had no children. And one day, after ten years of marriage, she fell off a cliff and died.

Such a strange way to leave the world. She fell off a cliff. What could be more final than that? Two miscarriages and a husband who was constantly unfaithful. What does a woman do? She falls off a cliff. Convenient.

I visited him after the bereavement but perhaps that is the wrong word to use. There was no feeling of 'bereavement' that I could see. All that he could say was that I should return to him and leave my husband and children as he had no place for 'another man's kids'. Oh, and could I bear children now? Was my age suitable? Or were my kids adopted?

My God! Leave my Akash for this monster who could not even feel emotion? Could speak like this barely one month after his wife was dead? What had I been saved from? Which power had saved me? It could have been me lying at the bottom of the cliff now.

I smiled, patted his hand and went back home. Certain things are not to be forgiven or forgotten. Leaving me all those years ago was forgivable. These things happen all the time. Not worth making a song and dance over. Not worth the price of newsprint or a read.

What he said that day was not. How he dealt with his wife's memory was not. How he spoke about my family was not. In a way, both of us, his wife and I, were abused.

Oh, what this monster needed was a child. He would love a child as he would never love another woman, and then because of that love he would know suffering. I prayed to Someone up there that he should have children. That would be revenge indeed. That would perhaps awaken him to feelings.

I kept up contact. He thought that I was still fascinated by him. Of course, I let him. Let him think that I had forgotten everything. Of how I was used all those years ago. Of how his family had spread malicious rumours about mine ... Of how he treated all women as pieces of flesh to be used at will.

He married Shelly when his first wife's ashes hardly had time to cool. 'Have a baby,' I cooed. 'You should you know.' 'But it must be a boy,' he stipulated.

You cannot lay down laws before fate. You cannot bend the wheel of karma. Someone had already decided that he was to have children. He did not tell me that Shelly was pregnant, but as I had told you, I knew.

And he had a son.

Flashing scarlet blooms cast red-gold shadows on the white walls of the hospital outside the cool maternity ward. Frangipani blossoms wafted down to my feet. And as I looked at the baby, something melted around my heart and I was free. Free of all thoughts of revenge. Free of Dev forever. Free to return to my loved ones, my beloved ones and continue in my happy life. ...

Bitterness does not remain. One day it is swept aside and you should grab that huge liberating wave and swing away ... I was rescued in more ways than one by the Someone that we all have by our side. Belief and faith is the same thing in the end and I had ample proof that Someone was looking after me and mine. Always.

I blew the babe a kiss as he slept and left the hospital. Outside, the birds sang a lullaby to the skies.

Amreeta Sen

Superannuation

In the silence of the living room of Flat No. 308 of the Vardhman Society in Noida, the last few words of his retirement speech echoed in Ashok's ears and his eyes were moist. 'Friends, I have a great house in Bhopal, where I will settle after retirement. I have my only son and his family living there. Please do visit me, I shall be honoured. Thank you very much for the party!'

When he and his wife Neeta reached their dream house in Bhopal, they were asked to adjust in the guestroom as their son and grandchildren had settled into the master and other bedrooms. Their son Nalin also told them that there was no space for their luggage and it would be kept in the outhouse. Neeta had collected paintings, curios and wall pieces as per the interiors of her dream house. She was hurt, but preferred peace, and so was magnanimous enough to take no cognisance of such minor issues. Neeta was a very pragmatic lady.

But things did not stop here. Either they were made to feel like intruders in their own house, or asked to pay for its maintenance. Ashok had planned a great retired life and had decided to work for an NGO, but now he actually needed one to help him instead. He tried his level best to compromise, but each day began with a new controversy.

One day, his son announced that he was going on vacation

to Europe. 'We'll be away for two weeks. Please get all the repairs done in that time,' the daughter-in-law said.

Ashok knew exactly what to do when their son and family were away.

In the next week he approached real estate agents, and without wasting much time, sold his dream house. He got an excellent deal. He spent just a fraction of the amount he got in buying a one-bedroom flat in Noida, and while their son was away on the vacation, Ashok and Neeta shifted with their baggage to their new apartment.

After two weeks, when their son and his family returned from a great holiday, they were thrilled to see a newly-painted house. But to their horror, a stranger walked out of house, handed over the keys of the outhouse to them and said, 'Your parents have sold this house to me and your luggage is lying in the outhouse. Kindly remove it as soon as possible as I have to renovate that area.' He also told them that their parents had instructed him not to give them their new address.

The silence in the Noida flat finally broke when Neeta, with her arms around Ashok, said lovingly, 'Darling, let's go out and have some Chinese food and celebrate the beginning of our new life.'

'Yes, let's,' Ashok replied happily.

Chitra Vashisht

Tarot

I was dumped. Overnight. Without so much as a 'by your leave'. And as he disappeared, so did I—and I realised I did not exist without being alive in 'his' eyes. I would awake in the mornings wanting the night and its oblivion to save me; and I would toss about at night, wanting the day and its distractions to start. Every task was just another shade of pain.

For the first time in my life, I felt the utter incapacitation of powerlessness. Where was that woman who lived life larger than life itself? What had she been reduced to? A mere version of her former self, with a mind dithering between calling the sharp slashes of betrayal 'a learning experience' and 'just blind stupidity'. Like a razor through my consciousness, I felt torn between two contrasting emotions; an inexplicable, intense love, and it's mutated opposite, a bitter, acidic hatred. I tried to make my weapons of anger my God; I even thought of revenge, but something, something warned me that if I allowed those weapons to win, I would be the one defeated.

I hated all this negativity inside of me. Its energy was so draining, demeaning. I had prided myself at living a life full of positive energy and optimism. And now, I was tormented by my own sense of humiliation and barrage of questions —

why did this happen? How could he do this? How was he? Was he well? And of course, let me be candid: the primary question—did he think of me? Ever?

All my spiritual background and years of attending satsangs, reading sacred and philosophical texts and imbibing the preaching of various gurus, seemed to come to nought. They ran the risk of remaining purely academic, for while I knew all the answers to my questions on an intellectual and spiritual level, actually believing in them was another matter altogether. Karma? What good was it doing me? How does one force the heart to not feel? How does one suppress the memories flooding the brain? How does one heal and move on?

Friends rallied around me of course, but I realised that my troubled spirit's healing lay in my hands and my hands alone.

I consciously made an effort to look inward and draw from the immense storehouse of peace and knowledge accumulated during my regular visits to satsangs. My connection with my Godself, intellectualised as it might have been, allowed me to turn the corner at that point, slowly but surely. Like planted seeds where the process takes place unseen, under the surface, and then, one fine day, voila! the sprouts start to show; the same happened to my state of consciousness. One fine morning, I actually awoke without thoughts of him in my mind!

And surprisingly, it was not my 'gyan' that allowed me to complete this shift, but a new ally—love! Yes! I fell in love again! A new love with all its accompanying feelings of passion and excitement! Yes, it was this new love that allowed me to not only release the past and emerge intact, but to be fulfilled in a way I had never dreamt of!

All it took was this one switch of focus, from trying to fill the self from outside, to finding it within. And it was all so simple! The answer lay not in any profound spiritual practices, nor in New Age meditation techniques, not even in a new round of satsangs, but in something more simple and attainable—a new hobby! A creative pursuit! Something I fell totally in love with and which brought me inexplicable joy. The esoteric had always drawn me, but I was so busy looking for fulfilment in the outside world, that I had completely negated this inner urge. And then I found tarot—or more accurately, tarot found me!

I was giving a lift to a friend's friend on my way to a tarot card reader for yet another reading. The acquaintance asked me why I didn't just learn the cards instead! I enrolled, more as a means to kill a few hours and to keep my mind from dwelling on the tortuous monotony of those unanswerable questions, than anything else. But soon my fascination grew and I felt that I wasn't running from myself every time I went for class, but towards a new self. The cards opened up a whole new world for me—my new date was the magician of the tarot deck, my new muse the high priestess card, and the Lovers was now a tarot card! And more literally too did the new world unlock, through the fascinating people I met who shared not only tarot, but so much of their self, that sharing took on a new meaning itself. After what seemed like forever, I felt alive again and empowered. I was once again staying up nights, but lost in unlocking the fascinating world of tarot. And yes, I was once again waking early, but to put pen to paper for something other than love letters. I embarked upon writing about all that I had learnt. And that was yet another love. . . .

And soon I realised there was nothing to remove, no pain that I needed to exorcise. There was only an increasingly fulfilled self. Yes, initially I was like a wine glass filled to the brim, so that even a jostle would empty me again. But even as this joie de vivre—for self, for others, for life—started to pour out, I turned that final corner. And thus what started as a tentative hobby rapidly snowballed into finding this wondrous, unique and fulfilled self. And she is still growing, and she is still oh so in love, and she does not wait for passion to call her and fix a date—she expands her horizons within!

Divyaa Kummar

The Clear Voice

What a thrilling moment that was! Four a.m. on 5 September 1986, at Mumbai International Airport, we were finally boarding a Pan Am flight, taking us to the wonderland of the US! Back then, the US was a dreamland, not just for me, an eighteen-year-old girl, but to all twenty-one of us in the Aavishkar group.

Aavishkar, a folk dance group from Ahmedabad, was representing Indian folk culture at seventeen different destinations in America. After one year of hard work, intense practice, growing enthusiasm and countless dreams, it was finally time to explore the fascinating and spectacular world of the west!

As we were a bunch of excited friends, an hour and a half passed just changing seats, settling down and gearing up for the much-awaited tour. Then we landed at the Karachi airport. Some disturbance at the entrance attracted my attention and I was aghast to see a tall, handsome man with a stony face, sharp features and ruthless expression in his eyes, pointing a gun at an airhostess! Three others followed him, all fully armed with ammunition; they took over our aircraft within minutes.

The entire cockpit crew had fled the plane, leaving 221 passengers at the mercy of ruthless terrorists and helpless airhostesses! This was followed by fifteen hours of trauma: predominantly consisting of watching the four of them going up and down the aisle with guns, and scared airhostesses looking at the frightened passengers helplessly. The only sounds were those of the children crying, women trying to console them and the terrorists shouting. The actions and the conversations of the terrorists were indicative of what they had in mind for us. They were trying to negotiate some sort of terms with the authorities. As the clock ticked, the expressions on their faces changed noticeably from ruthlessness to frustration, and finally anger. Clearly, their demands had not been met.

As if the situation wasn't bad enough, due to fuel loss and the hours that we had been onboard the plane, the air-conditioning quit. The aircraft was now even more suffocating. The lights started to become dimmer and finally came darkness. This was immediately followed by a prayer in a language that was alien to me, and then came the indiscriminate firing, explosions of hand grenades, followed by loud, deafening screams and shouts all around. The open fire, combined with the darkness, led to complete chaos and a stampede of unruly passengers trying to escape while they still could.

Suddenly, my feet felt hot and soon that was the only thing I could feel. In the next flash, my friend Roopal, sitting next to me, shrieked with pain and almost lost consciousness. Another friend Urmi and I grabbed Roopal and joined the chaos in the pursuit of freedom. The two of us could barely manage ourselves, but we made sure Roopal was with us all along.

Suddenly we found ourselves stepping down. What I saw was an unimaginable sight. We were on the wing of the aircraft, where an airhostess was helping people jump from the wing to the tarmac below, which was around twenty-one feet from the ground.

But out in the open, feeling the first gush of fresh air in fifteen hours, I became more aware of some warm feeling in my feet. I looked down and was shocked to see blood oozing out ... I turned to Roopal, and saw that she was bleeding profusely. At this point, I decided not to jump, and told the airhostess that none of us could jump in our present states. She guided us back into the aircraft all the way to the back, where there was an emergency chute, which we could use to slide down to the ground.

We dared to make our way back into that aircraft again, and though we had been holding on to each other, in the chaos, we lost each other. I somehow managed to reach the chute. I heard the airhostess asking me to simply sit and slide. I was terrified and hesitated, but I was pushed and found myself heading down with great speed and landing with a big *thud* on the ground.

That was it. The moment my feet touched the ground, I knew that they were severely injured, and it would be impossible for me to move. Behind me, another girl slid down. She asked me to get up so she could do the same and there were people waiting to come down the chute to escape from the aircraft! I begged the girl to help me get up as I simply could not do it myself.

I managed to get up with her support with great difficulty, only to realise that I could not walk on my own. I could not leave her hand and she, a complete stranger, supported me. We walked very slowly on the tarmac towards the airport. People around us were frantically running, and we heard people shouting, 'They are coming again'. Perhaps the terrorists, who had run out of ammunition, were also running with us to try and escape. But the petrified people were too scared to think of anything or realise what was happening. That shout made all those around us panic and run even faster. My unknown friend and I exchanged a look of desperation.

She let go of my hand and started running ... I was left there, unable to move in the midst of all that turmoil. Around me were passengers frantically running forward to save their lives shouting, 'Run, run, they are coming again'.

Behind me were the terrorists. In front of me, near the airport building, I could spot a line of gun-toting Pakistani commandoes. I felt a chilling fear down my spine! 'Janki, you don't have many options. Just run. I know you can make it,' a voice from inside guided me. I obeyed that inner voice which was so loud and clear, which made all the noise around suddenly fade away. I found a power within me that transcended all the pain, and I took my first step forward; I could do it. Then the next step, and finally, I was running! I ran all the way from the middle of the tarmac to the airport. As I neared the commandoes, I was in a state of nothingness. ...

I was directed to the lounge where I saw familiar faces, all silenced and in a state of shock. I finally slumped onto a couch next to a friend, and could not get up thereafter. I was later taken to Jinnah Hospital.

The next time I walked was after three months.

Janki Vasant

The Open Ground of Middle Age

Confined within domesticity,
Supposedly fulfilled by motherhood,
By wifeliness, by duty to family,
A woman forgets there may be spaces
In a life, some prairies wide and free.
When freedom comes, can she forget
The past that held her fast in subtle chains?
Suddenly this vast space looms ahead,
Unlooked for. That protective cloak
That smothered me, kept me
From my true self, is gone. But now,
Here is the woman's paradox:
In freedom there is a different lack.
Yet I do not want my old life back:
It is gone forever, a lost horizon.
I stand exposed, at the very centre
Of the open ground of middle age,
Afraid, but not wishing for old chains
To anchor me, because I wish to grow.

(Written at the beginning of a relationship)

Jane Bhandari

The White Hair

Among the bushes of side-burns
lay that meandering white hair
just around my right ear,
giving me so much of fear.
On the roll was
my contemplation,
my day-dreaming
as I started thinking
Of those teeth
that would be gone,
Of those wrinkles
that would be born
and ...
Of those bones
that would be weak
and no longer hold up this geek.

A NEW LEASE

As my thoughts crept into the grey days,
with the dusky sun burying its rays,
I looked at life ...
those 'young', old days,
And before I could cry,
I smiled at myself ...
looking into the mirror
that unveiled my hair
All I saw was just a thread
playing around, grey and dead
And all I saw was the time I still had
and a life, young and red!

Ankur Garg

When My Heart Gave Up

I woke up groggy and with a severe pain in my legs. I felt totally confused and out of place. I could barely see my daughter Nitya's face, but heard her voice, 'Hi Mama, are you feeling alright?'

I looked around, trying to remember how I had ended up in a hospital room. The last memory I had was of me watering the plants in my garden. I struggled to speak, but the words wouldn't come out.

Nitya held my restless hands, 'It's alright Mom. You had a bypass surgery. Dad just left for work and Anand left for college. You have to be in this ICU for a couple of days. Then they'll be shifting you to their regular rooms for a few more days. We'll take turns to stay with you. You really gave us all a scare, Mom!'

I don't think I heard her after her second sentence. 'Bypass surgery!' I croaked. 'That is not funny, Nitya!'

There were tears in her eyes, 'I'm not kidding, Mom. You had a heart attack. Why didn't you tell me you were not well?'

I tried to smile, 'How could I tell you, when I didn't know it myself? Who brought me to the hospital? I can't seem to remember anything.'

'Rama Aunty saw you from her backyard. Thank god she

remembered to call 911 before rushing to you. If they had been even a few minutes late . . .' Her voice choked and she left the room, leaving me to my thoughts.

She came back after a few minutes, voice composed and a smile on her face, 'I'm so glad you're alright Mom. We all have to take better care of our health. You stay at home and you had a heart attack. Dad, Anand and I go out and work and study. Just imagine the stress we are under!'

The next few days of recovery were slow and painful. It felt like I'd been hit with a ton of bricks. It was a great comfort to have my family and friends by my side. Everybody seemed shocked that I'd had a heart attack. The doctors were trying to figure out what could have caused it. It took us some time to realise that I'd been having lots of symptoms prior to the attack. I'd not been sleeping well and would always be tired. I had just dismissed them as day-to-day problems. My neck and shoulder frequently hurt and, occasionally, when I complained of chest pain, my doctor had dismissed it as indigestion. I had been asked to get more physical exercise and had taken up gardening, which could also be very stressful. I'd also ignored the fact that my mother had died of a heart attack.

We all think and feel that we are immune to anything really bad happening to us. I guess I was not an exception. From the day we can understand things, we've been taught to take care of everybody, but us. When I was a daughter, I was told that I should learn to cook and take care of the house. Then I became a wife, and was expected to compromise my feelings and needs for my husband and in-laws. When my children were born, nobody had to tell me anything as my maternal instinct took over.

Now, please don't get me wrong. I love and cherish my family. I've absolutely no regrets about any of my life-decisions. Then, why is it that when I ask for some appreciation, all I get back is, 'If it's hard for you, just imagine how hard it is for me?'

Why is it that, after forty-five years of mini heart-breaks, when my heart finally gave up, I still get the same response from my daughter?

*

I'm back at my house, surrounded by my loving family and friends. My husband, daughter and son have taken time off from their busy schedules to take care of me. It's just been a few weeks since I've been discharged, but I've been trying to get back to my routine. I can see that they're all getting restless to return to their work and college. After all, they did take very good care of me and now life must move on. Everything seems to be the same, but I can still feel a major change. I've realised that the only person I can really change is myself.

I've started listening to my body's needs. I exercise more, and I try to eat healthier. I spend more time talking (not gossiping) to my friends about my feelings. Trust me; talking is a wonderful outlet to all of our complicated emotions. I'm very regular with my medical check-ups. I spend so much of my time trying to keep everybody in my family healthy. Surely, I can take out some time to keep *myself* healthy.

As for all those lovely comments that still keep coming my way, I've just decided to ignore them and try not to take them to my heart. As I said before, the only person I can really change is myself!

Sangeetha Narayan

5
GIVE AND GROW

When we feel love and kindness toward others, it not only makes others feel loved and cared for, but it helps us also to develop inner happiness and peace.

—H.H. the Dalai Lama

A Little Love to Spare

Thanks to my husband's transferable job, moving home every few years has become an accepted part of my life. Packing and shifting certainly posed minor problems, particularly when the children were in school and college. But the positive side—meeting new people, seeing new places, encountering new experiences—have all made it worthwhile.

Of the many brief associations made over the years, a few remained in touch and evolved into close friends. Some drifted into the abysses of time, till we suddenly met each other again, while others gradually faded into the past and became a part of nostalgic memories. But the young girl who fleetingly came into my life many years ago was different.

I had befriended Divya in the ancient land of the Tigris and Euphrates. Her father was a senior colleague of my husband and we were among the few families who had decided to brave the uncertainties of war-torn Iraq and live in Baghdad. The assignment lasted barely two-and-a-half years. The memories will last a lifetime.

Though Divya was Indian, not Iraqi, understanding her had been difficult. Being completely deaf, her speech—guttural and indistinct—was the language of the hearing-impaired. But somehow I wanted to overcome this communication barrier and know her a little better.

I had noticed our inability to understand her often made her take refuge in a cocoon of isolation. It was thus with some hesitation that I attempted to befriend the withdrawn teenager. Total ignorance of how to behave with someone with a disability made me unsure at first. After her initial diffidence to my overtures of friendship, it became apparent that Divya was far more adept at comprehending my attempts to communicate than I was at deciphering hers!

It took time and perseverance to establish a modicum of familiarity. I didn't really get an opportunity to become very close or intimate, but those fleeting months of interaction with her gave me glimpses of a hitherto unknown world. A world that was an integral part of the one I was so familiar with, yet had no conception about. Without realising it, she had awakened in me a need to delve further.

My chance came when we fled Iraq towards the end of 1990—the US threats of annihilation and destruction rumbling too close for comfort. Posted at Kolkata, I identified an organisation doing commendable work for children and young adults with cerebral palsy, and offered my services.

Wanting to work with the disabled was one thing. Being able to do so was another matter altogether. Divya was my only experience of interacting with a disabled child. Warnings were sounded that working with challenged children was anything but easy. Not because it would be physically exhausting, but because it was emotionally draining. Nevertheless, I didn't want to give up even before trying.

The first day will always remain imprinted in my mind. I would not be completely honest if I denied my initial apprehensions. But entering the classroom of four- to six-year-olds, the voluble greeting I received from Arijit dispelled all my doubts. The fact that his welcome comprised more of meaningless sounds than actual words did little to diminish his warmth.

A complete novice, I gradually learnt under the guidance of the trained teachers. But it was the children who provided the practical lessons—childlike Simita helping her friend in the toilet; unsteady Samrat carefully pushing the wheelchair of a less mobile friend; generous Kavita sharing her biscuits with a deprived peer. Of course this willingness to help was overdone occasionally. Like Basant who would insist on providing the answers no matter what, refusing to give his slower classmates a chance!

Reluctant to commit myself to all five working days of the week, I started off going there twice a week. However, I had not counted on how involved I would become. When at home, my thoughts would be with the children—Abdul practising walking on his crutches with tears of pain; Pinky correctly identifying the photographs of her class friends; Rana differentiating between blue and green; Nafiz doing a silent namaste without being prompted; Chiku exuberantly wishing everyone 'good morning' and 'see you'. In less than a year, I was there all five days.

In the beginning, my attention was focused only on the eighteen or so little girls and boys in my assigned class. With time, my rather insular attitude changed as I gradually came to know and became familiar with many others. No regular interaction. Just a word, a smile, a touch.

I had volunteered thinking about how I would effect a change in many lives. Of helping little ones physically, of assisting older children with studies, of solving dilemmas unique to adolescents and young adults, of supporting distraught parents come to terms. Never in my wildest imagination did I have any conception of the tremendous impact they would make in my life instead.

I learnt the true essence of helping when I saw a handicapped youngster unhesitatingly assist a more disabled friend. I comprehended the spirit of compassion when I witnessed an older parent reassure another still struggling to come to terms with reality. I understood what thoughtfulness meant when a quadriplegic young adult gave away a new sweater to her old mother despite being in a torn one herself. I discovered how love could be given unstintingly, no questions asked.

My association with Divya all those years ago had made me realise how little I knew about youngsters like her. And that understanding them just needed an open mind and a willing heart. I had a little love to spare. So I decided to share it among those children. Never did I imagine it being such an excellent investment. How else does one explain the unconditional love that I got back in return—many times over?

Anjana Jha

Angels Don't Always Have Wings

It had been a soul-lifting and yet heart-crushing evening because I had just returned from a cousin's place where she and her two young, pretty daughters had been sweet, but hadn't asked me to stay back for dinner. I walked back to the Mandvi bus stop nearby and as I stood there, mentally working out if I could afford a bus ride or a light snack, my heart sank to start pounding against my knees. I had absolutely no money!

Okay, said the battle-weary fighter within me, let me first reach my room at 41 Pratap Gunj and then I could join any buddy walking down to The Wien, the mess where we had our accounts for meals. But walking from Mandvi to Pratap Gunj was beyond me physically, at that point.

Stricken and almost defeated, I stood there petrified, as bus after bus to my area came and went. I didn't have a single paisa on me, this trickle of realisation soon sounded like a waterfall too deafening to bear. When the Mandvi tower clock struck 9 p.m., a streak of pure panic frothed its way through my entire being—time was running short. The mess would close if I didn't reach quickly.

Finally, with a do-or-die look on my face, I hailed an auto-rickshaw cruising by. It stopped. I climbed in casually and said, '41 Pratap Gunj.' The driver mumbled something with an affirmative tone and I imagined he said, 'Yes, I know.'

A hungry tummy can cause hallucinations, I thought. But wonder of wonders—while I was engaged in working out a scheme to borrow money from my very nice neighbours to pay for my rickshaw fare, he had driven his vehicle steadily and had brought me right to my doorstep.

'How much?' I asked, with that old sinking feeling in my heart returning now.

'Sir, how can I take money from you?' said the dark, young man, grinning. His face was in deep shadows, the street lights had gone off, his own headlights were too dim. Without waiting for my reaction, he sped off.

To this day, the identity of this Good Samaritan who bailed me out from a horrid situation remains a blessed mystery. With perfect hindsight, I now recall that he had said he knew where I lived, he had not activated his fare meter, and he had painstakingly kept his face in the shadows all along.

Ever since then, I have given lifts to needy folks from time to time. People have pooh-poohed my goodness, because I have given lifts to stranded women on lonesome roads, something a car driver would shirk from by instinct. I have done that and much more because I have to get this obligation off my shoulders. I have also realised that angels don't always have wings—they roam about amongst us, just like you or me.

Max Babi

Assignment

My mother always says, before sending people to earth, God assigns a special cause to everyone. Living a life like millions of others, I often wondered what could be my special cause. ...

The cab stopped at the Jubilee Hills crossing. It was an ordinary afternoon, irritatingly hot even in November. However, my well-reputed company takes care of its employees and provides us with AC cars all year round. I was lost in the music of *Careless Whispers* with my eyes shut, when I heard a faint knock. I opened my eyes. I saw a dirty woman knocking the window of my cab. Though a little irritated at the disturbance, I paused the music and rolled down the window to give some coins to the woman. It was mercilessly hot outside and I felt a little pang for the tiny baby strapped around her waist.

'Madam, I am not a beggar. I am here to sell this. It is only ten rupees. It pumps real water,' the woman said. I looked at the dirty jute bag she was carrying on one shoulder and the baby wrapped around her waist. The baby looked as if he (I assumed) had not been given a bath for weeks: dusty face, uncombed hair, and a pathetically flowing nose. And if that was not enough, the baby was crying at the top of his voice. The woman took out several toys from her jute bag and tried to sell me something.

Scorching heat, a traffic jam, a waiting boss—the last thing I wanted on earth was the toy hand pump that this lady was trying to make me buy.

'I don't want it,' I said a little rudely.

'Madam, take it for your children,' she insisted, her voice getting desperate.

'I don't have any,' I said.

'Take it as a gift for someone dear to you. Take it for just eight rupees, madam.' She would simply not let go.

To get rid of her, and to return to George Michael, I extracted a ten-rupee note to buy the toy.

As I was taking the toy from the woman, her baby extended his palm towards it; but by the time he could reach it, it was in my possession. I thought I saw helplessness in his eyes. It was the same helplessness I had felt innumerable times before, when I had not got something that I had desired intensely.

I returned the toy to the woman, saying, 'It's a gift for your child.' I can't say if the mother was more happy or the child. She raised her hand and said something in Telugu. Then she gave the toy to the baby. Instantly the tears stopped and a bright smile flashed across the dusty face. Oddly, he didn't look that dirty any more. I can't say that he looked any less adorable than my little nieces or nephews.

'What did she say?' I asked Rama, my Hyderabadi colleague.

'She blessed you. She prayed to Tirupati swami that you also come across people with a heart like yours, and may the Lord realise all your wishes.'

The signal turned green and the cab started. I realised then, that perhaps making babies smile was the special task assigned to me.

It's been around a year now, and I have drawn twelve pay cheques since then. However I spend or save it, nothing gives me more pleasure than buying a little toy and passing it over to a little child, covered in mud and playing on the footpath barefoot. They don't care which brand that toy is and what its price is. They accept it with all their heart and give me a priceless smile in return.

Avantika Debnath

Blood Donation

A few years back, a friend of mine, Meera, suffered kidney failure and was admitted to the medical college for dialysis. Before dialysis, she needed at least three units of blood. I and another friend, Lovey, offered ourselves, but we still needed a third donor. We were touched and felt really proud when Lovey's eighteen-year-old daughter Belmeira said that she would like to help out.

At the medical college, Lovey and I went in first to have our blood drawn. When it was Belmeira's turn, the doctor informed us that Meera could be transfused with only two units that day. I could sense that Belmeira felt disappointed. She had so much wanted to do her bit for her mother's friend. We were about to leave the blood bank when we saw an old man in conversation with the nurse on duty. She was trying her best to make him understand that he could not *buy* blood at this bank and only donors were entertained. We could tell that the old villager was tearful and at the point of breaking down. We learnt that his son was to undergo dialysis too, but the hospital wasn't accepting him as a donor because of his advanced age and frail health. He had no friends or acquaintances in Lucknow and didn't know whom to turn to. With that the old helpless father broke down.

Then a wonderful thing happened. Belmeira reached out

for the old man's hand. 'Don't worry baba,' she said, 'I'll give blood for your son.' She turned to us and both Lovey and I nodded our consent. Then this young girl, with a heart of gold, went ahead to give her blood, to a complete stranger, someone she would never meet. When she came out of the lab she walked over to the old father and gave him a hug. To this day I remember the expression of gratitude on the father's face and the smile on Belmeira's.

Rehana Ali

Clapping for God

I had been to several gatherings where people pray in a silent, reverent manner. It was on my friend's insistence that I went to this particular place with a slightly different ambience, where one could pray as animatedly as one wanted.

During the sermon, I noticed an elderly couple accompanied by their mentally-challenged son sitting in front of me. While the son sat and watched the proceedings, the parents prayed devoutly; they seemed anguished and worried. During a break, the speaker came on his rounds and I heard them tell him that they were concerned about their son. The preacher assured them that their son was special and God had a plan for him, which would be revealed in His time.

As the prayer service continued, the preacher asked the people to sing and praise God and the crowd followed his advice without any discomfort. The son was quite oblivious to what was happening around him. At one point, the speaker asked everybody to stand up and clap for God. It was then that I noticed that the boy was not able to stand up properly—evidently he had some problem with his legs.

The boy gestured to his parents that he too wanted to stand up and clap, but his parents, aware of the discomfort it would cause him, told him that God would not mind if he sat and clapped also adding, 'You are special to him'. But the boy kept on insisting that he too wanted to clap like the others. His parents gave in, and with the help of their support, he stood up and began clapping like the rest of us. His face betrayed occasional flashes of pain at the effort, but he continued clapping with more enthusiasm than all the others.

We started clapping louder to cheer the boy on. His face turned even more radiant and I saw the parents' eyes water as they looked proudly at their son and then with gratitude towards all of us. At that moment we were all one!

I had come to pray for yet another thing that I thought was mandatory for a good life. Watching that little boy struggle even for basic routine tasks sent waves of remorse through me. I forgot all my selfish 'wants' and instead prayed for the happiness of that special boy. I am sure that every single person in that room did exactly that.

One cannot help but realise how petty we are complaining about our issues, when He has woven so many beautiful stories of strength and inspiration around us. For the child, the simple act of clapping for God was all that mattered, and that made me understand that life is indeed far more beautiful than what we make it to be.

Beryl Kunjavu

For the Tsunami

Trying to do my bit for the tsunami victims, I had gone with a group of friends to collect money from the public. After getting cheques (from relatives, mostly) and having exhausted all known resources, we hit the streets, tin boxes in hand.

'I don't want to see any pairs. Each of us will take a separate corner,' I said, with more courage than I felt.

I found a safe corner at Town Hall square. I would walk into the traffic when it stopped for a red light, and jump out just before it turned green.

'Tsunami mate!' I would say, jingling the box. ('Mate' is 'for' in Gujarati.)

Those who looked back at my face, my eyes, more often than not reached into their pockets. The box took in coins, even some ten-rupee notes. I always said a cheerful 'thank you'.

After an hour, I realised that it was passengers in auto rickshaws who were more eager to put cash in my box. Those in cars avoided my eyes. So it's true, I thought. The middle class is much more generous than the rich.

And then, horror of horrors, a beggar attached himself to me, and started following me around. A middle-aged, dirty, if-he-could-beg, he-could-work kind of beggar. I became extremely hassled. Should I confront him or should I take a tea break? What would I say if I confronted him? More importantly, what would he say to me?

The lights turned green suddenly and I stepped back on the square.

I turned around to see the beggar smiling a 'hello comrade' at me.

'Tsunami mate?' he asked me.

I nodded, slightly unnerved by his sweet smile.

He took out a five hundred rupee note and slid it in my box, and walked away!

Thank you, comrade. Thank you for the donation, and for the respect you awakened in me for all beings.

Manjushree Abhinav

Forgotten Names

When Bini died, I didn't go to see her. I could not look to the end of the street where her mom kept her body and was crying. I didn't see Bini when she was alive either, but her mom Aduri used to do the dishes at our place for a meagre sum of thirty rupees a month. This is way back in the '70s, so I guess she could make do with whatever amount she earned then. I just hope she could. I don't know. Like I never could get myself to go up to her and console her for her daughter's death, I couldn't look at the little hut they used to live in. The hut was so low, one would have to crawl inside. I would walk past. But I was pretty civil to Aduri. In fact, I loved it when she came over to clean the house. I wouldn't have to study then. I would just follow her from one room to another and listen to her speak. I could speak her dialect. And she definitely took pride in that.

My mother, when she found out about Bini's ailment, paid for her treatment at our local hospital. But they couldn't save her. I forget what happened to her. And cannot ask my mother either, because she too passed away some years back. Believe me, she has taken away with her some awesome recipes of dishes that I grew up on. I miss her.

Aduri in Bengali means someone who is loved and cuddled all the time. Our Aduri definitely didn't have time for that.

She was too busy working as household help in some ten houses all through the day. And in the night her drunk husband would either beat her up or try to get her pregnant again. That is, unless she was already pregnant.

She was always pregnant. When I remembered Bini's death (just the faint wail of Aduri sitting at the corner of the street in front of her body) last night, I placed a hand on Aaron. He was trying one of his Z poses in his sleep as usual. He can be a great contortionist. One just has to make him sleep during the show.

And then I wondered how Aduri would have felt at her death. She couldn't cry her heart out . . . she didn't have time. And then she had her other children to feed. Her eldest was a boy, probably my age, a guy who played all day. Believe me, I envied him. I met him later when I was in senior school. I had gone to one of the local hooch shops to buy liquor for the first time in my life. I and some friends of mine went up to the shop and bought some country liquor, saying it was for our dads! As if the guy selling the stuff cared who we were buying it for. I don't remember how much it was for, but we fell short by ten rupees. And this fellow, Aduri's son, lent that money to me.

I never saw him after that. I eventually left Durgapur and then moved on to Banaras, Delhi, and then Bangalore, and forgot all about him until last night. I remembered him because I remembered Bini. Or her death. But I don't remember his name. He must be grown up now, working somewhere. And I calculated how much I owe him. Going by the Sensex, way back in '79 at 100 points, I owe him a lot today. The Sensex has breached the 15,000 mark, and those ten rupees would be . . .? Rs 15,000.

I called up my friend in Durgapur today. He said he will find out about Aduri. She must be really old, probably still working as hard, scrubbing plates, mopping floors . . . how much do we actually owe her? Can I buy her a retirement package? Not with Rs 15,000 for sure. You can buy just a couple of standing wooden speakers from Sonodyne with that kind of money. And I've been eyeing the Sonodyne Sonus speakers for the last three years now.

What if I say I don't have that money? Will the wail stop coming back to me?

Arijit Ghosh

From a Teacher's Desk

'I'm surrounded by a group of sprightly ten-year-olds.'
'Miss . . . me too.'
'Please write my name also.'
'Will we see many tigers in Bandhavgarh?'
'My father said yes too.'
'Wow! We'll have fun. Miss, will you allow friends to sleep in the same room in the hotel?'
'We'll have to wear brown or dull-green T-shirts. Bright colours will scare the tigers away.'
'And don't squeal when you see the tiger. He'll jump on you,' I can sense this one's imagination is beginning to run wild.

Their childish enthusiasm and excitement makes me smile and want to hug each one of them. Then I notice her. She is looking on wistfully. A small little girl, her tunic, a size too large, hanging loosely on her thin frame.

'Rinika, aren't you coming too?'
'No!'

I'm taken aback by her brusque reply. There's something here that I don't know. But dare I probe? It seems I don't need to. With childish innocence and not a trace of malice, the others provide me with the answer.

Miss, Rinika can't go. She's a foundationer.' As if that one word explains everything.

I have a lump forming in my throat. Rinika's head sinks lower. She grips the edge of my table to keep her little hands from trembling, but her lips droop and a tear falls on the table top.

I make a sudden decision. I put an arm around her thin waist and draw her close.

'So what? Mrs Abraham has said that Rinika is such a good girl she has to go on this excursion to see the tiger.'

'Yipee!' the children cheer in unison.

'Miss, I don't have a mom and dad to pay for the trip.' A small, trembling voice.

'Silly! This is a like a prize for being so good' I'm hoping my Principal will forgive me for taking this liberty.

The beginning of a smile plays on her lips. Dare she believe me? Dare she hope? Her friends hug her and I marvel at the innocence of childhood. Brutally cruel one moment and disarmingly warm the next.

'Now off with all of you. Take this list to Matron. She'll help you to pack your bags.'

I see her skipping all the way out of the room with the others, her pigtails bobbing happily.

'You did right Rehana. And what are *you* crying for, stupid girl?'

I want to hug her but it won't do for a teacher to be seen hugging the Principal, and that too in her office.

Rehana Ali

Moment of Clarity

I was in a car, getting a lift to the railway station. My train was leaving in two hours. We planned to have dinner in Swati, let the brat ride a small car or play a video game, maybe have a coffee, and then head to the station. So we were in no hurry. And my eyes were wide open.

Nirali, a friend, was explaining to my son, Pavan, why he should sit at the back, when I saw a man raising a big bamboo stick to hit a woman sitting on the roadside.

I closed my eyes.

'What the hell is that man doing?' Nirali asked.

'Oh, thank god, he is just threatening to hit her,' I said, when I saw the bamboo stick stop midair.

'Can we do something?' Nirali asked.

'Stop the car. I will get out.'

'Be careful.'

A sparse crowd was beginning to gather. The man, who I later learnt was a guard at a building nearby, was hurling obscenities at the woman, waving his stick in the air. The woman, with matted hair and in rags, was holding a plastic bottle to her mouth and looking back at the man. Although she seemed to be almost cowering, she did not look scared.

I was behind the man. I gently touched his shoulder, and got him to lower his stick.

'She is completely mad!' he kept repeating. I nodded.

'She throws stones at people. She threw a stone at me. At my back! For no reason! She threw stones at that auto-rickshaw! Ask the driver. She is completely mad!'

I looked at the lady in question. She had a semicircle of stones near her feet.

I assured him that we would get rid of her, got him to leave the scene, and told the crowd to get lost.

Then I sat on a bench near the woman and called Nirali.

'Do you know any institution that would take her in?' I asked her.

'I think I do. Meanwhile, why don't you get her something to eat? She might be hungry.'

I went to a shop next door and bought some dhoklas and a bottle of water. But to give them to her, I would have to risk those stones.

The semicircle of stones had closed to form a circle. That must be a good sign, I thought, and sat next to her to offer her the food.

Huge black eyes looked me over with suspicion. Then she took a bougainvillea flower, put it in a small plastic glass and put it in front of me. I took the glass and said cheers.

And then she attacked the food. Boy, was she hungry. No wonder she was throwing stones. I stood up and saw my friend smiling at us.

'I have called a friend who knows someone who will come,' said Nirali.

'Cool. Where is Pavan?' I asked.

'I have locked him in the car. You better go and sit with him. I will wait here.'

'Ai, what is in the glass?' the brat asked me as I opened the car door.

'This is a bougainvillea flower,' I told him.

'Who gave it to you?'

'A moment of clarity gave it to me.'

'I see.'

Manjushree Abhinav

Music of a Stolen Symphony

It's a late night on the streets of New York. Larger-than-life size billboards come alive with their glitz, trying to make you want things that you don't really need. Up ahead, I notice a homeless man who doesn't have the things he really does need. Ironic.

'Gift-size chocolate bar, one dollar, one dollar,' he says, while showing a candy bar to people walking by. He's rejected. 'Just one dollar.' Rejected again. 'Candy bar, candy bar for you,' he shows it to a child walking with her mom. The mom jerks her kid away and moves on.

They say that the homeless are used to taking rejections, but seeing the charades ahead of me, I can't help but feel sorry for him. As I stand next to him, shoulder to shoulder, I pause to see if he will try to sell me the candy. He doesn't. I turn to him and ask, 'Hey there, buddy. How are you?'

He looks me straight in the eye, as if startled at my directness. Maybe it is because I am ten minutes early for my dinner meeting, but I feel like I am in no rush at all. 'How are you doing today?' I repeat my question.

We start talking. A Hispanic guy named 'Hecttttauur', with somewhat dirty clothes, many missing teeth and alcohol on his breath. Hector tells me his two-minute autobiography, of how he used to be happily married and doing theatre until life threw him a few curve balls. Now he's disgruntled, disillusioned and alone on the streets.

In his right hand, Hector is holding a white plastic bag, in his left is the bar of chocolate. He's almost forgotten about it, until I ask, 'So, where did you get the candy bar?' I mean, I'm not trying to put him to shame (because both of us knew that he stole it) but I want him to ground himself in the space of truth ... even if it is only for that moment.

For the first time, Hector looks down at the ground and says in a softer voice, 'I stole it.' I don't want to pass judgment on his action, so I am silent. After a moment, he continues as if he's talking to a long-lost brother—'But what am I supposed to do? Life is so hard. I can't even survive out here, so I gotta do what I gotta do.' His eyes are still looking to the ground and I'm just holding the space of silence.

I pull out my wallet, spontaneously. 'Hey buddy, you were selling this for a dollar right?' Now, he's silent. 'Here's a dollar for your candy bar. But this is what I want you to do with the candy bar—I want you to give it freely, with an open heart, to someone you don't know.' I place a gold-coloured dollar coin that I've received as change from the train ticket booth.

'Just give it?' he replies as if it's a novel concept to him. 'Yeah, give it away. You receive a lot when you give,' I say with a heartfelt smile.

Almost like a child, he innocently counters—'But will they punch me if I give it away?'

Huh? It takes a good five seconds to process that question. Who would worry about being punched when giving? I realise that the concept of giving is so foreign to Hector, he doesn't even know what to expect. I can't believe it. I almost have tears in my eyes. It's one thing to be hurting because you don't have the basic necessities of life, but what poverty to not know the feeling of selfless giving!

'No, no, Hector. When you give, you don't get hurt. It will expand you. Whoever you give to will be happy and you will be happier because of that,' I tell him. Hector trusts me, by now. 'But you've got to give it away, okay?'

'Okay,' he says.

That bar of chocolate, Hershey's Symphony, is still in Hector's left hand. But now it is almost as if he has found the music in his stolen symphony.

Nipun Mehta

Reach Out and Help Someone

This is something that I grew up hearing from the good old Irish nuns who taught us. How true this actually is in the larger scheme of things, came home to me the day I met a very young, recently widowed girl with a young child.

Previously a bubbly youngster, a pampered wife, looked after and taken care of in every possible way, she sat before me completely broken, dejected, with a vacant look, seemingly as if life had stopped completely!

I could empathise with her, could well understand the dilemmas in her mind, which no amount of solace provided by anyone could ease or erase. What rose in me was a strong urge to protect her and help her. That feeling persisted and nagged me more with time, and I couldn't understand how to go about it. So I began by simply chatting about mundane things, and over a period of time, began to build a rapport with her. Perhaps, with time, she began to see me as a sounding board and as someone who was living life on her own terms, and the thought that she could do it too began to take root in her own mind.

In all my sessions / meetings / interactions with her, I wanted her to realise that the strength to overcome has to come from within oneself only, and one has to begin to draw on that inner reservoir.

Once we became comfortable with each other, I nagged her to stop and think about very basic things, like looking forward to the day, enjoying the morning newspaper and a good cup of tea, spending some time in front of her clothes cupboard deciding what to wear! Believe me, these went a long way in restoring her self-worth and she soon began to do things that she wanted to. Once she surprised me by baking a chocolate cake because she remembered I liked chocolates. It really touched me and had me crying!

When I saw her begin to drive and sort out paper work, it gave me immense satisfaction. I knew she had a long way to go, but at least a small start had been made. Generally, the first step is the most difficult one, but once taken, the momentum increases.

I also realised that the help we extend to others not only benefits them, but makes us grow too. For, wonderfully, I felt myself healed too—I had lost my husband a few years back to cancer.

Ruma Purkayashta

Small Things with Great Love

Mother Teresa often said: we cannot do great things, but only small things with great love; and small things have great results.

Our elders followed this principle in whatever way they could. From the time I was very small, I remember seeing my mother diligently put aside food for dogs and birds, and for a Brahmin and the sweeper. I remember the joy I used to feel when my mother asked me to give them the share that was set aside—inculcating in me the habit of sharing without uttering one word on why we should be doing it, and letting me experience the joy of giving myself.

Maybe this sharing was rooted in the belief that if you do good to others in times of distress, God sends help through messengers. She had implicit faith in God. Her mantra was, 'Do your best and leave the rest to God'.

Did she have a premonition of things to come? My father was a factory owner prior to Partition, and employed twenty-five to thirty workers. But overnight, with Partition, he became a refugee. He had to flee for the safety of his life and that of his family. Like many others, we had to leave behind our belongings and our homes, where our ancestors had lived for generations. We crossed the newly-demarcated border of Pakistan into Indian territory. We were on the road, without shelter, without any money. We were not sure where our next meal would come from.

But we found our messengers.

One philanthropist in Abhor Mandi would boil a big kadai of moong dal in the morning and one kadai of black gram in the evening. He would distribute it generously to the needy. There would be a serpentine queue of refugees to receive this dole. I cannot forget how much that food meant to the likes of us.

With heartfelt gratitude, we moved away from Abhor to Delhi in a goods train that was carrying coal, as my father had a few contacts over there. He wanted to explore opportunities there and hoped for help from his friends.

One of my father's business acquaintances in Delhi offered my father Rs 500, a princely sum for us in our time of crisis. This changed the course of our life. My father used his skills to craft sieves of the finest grade to convert wheat flour into maida. This worked. He could turn out maida of acceptable standard for use by bakeries. Since it was manually made, only a limited quantity could be produced, but this set the ball rolling.

We don't have to move mountains; even small acts can go to great lengths to change the lives of the recipients. What is in it for us? Why, the satisfaction of having done something without any expectations in return.

L.K. Baweja

The Gift of Sight

When I returned from my fifteen-day vacation outside Jamshedpur, the first thing I did was enquire whether there had been any eye donations at Roshni while I was away. I was told a pair of eyes was received from Mrs Sundari, who had donated her husband's eyes.

Roshni is an organisation that I founded along with some of my friends to promote eye donation in Jamshedpur. We had to work day in and day out, giving talks, distributing pledge forms, registering the names of potential donees (who are chosen by ophthalmologists for corneal transplantation), accompanying the doctors to a donor's house for removal of eyes from the dead body, etc.

Mrs Sundari and her husband had visited my house a few years back. After initial inquiries, they conveyed their wish to pledge their eyes. They told me that they were really lucky that there was an organisation in Jamshedpur to make use of their eyes after their death. They filled up the forms meticulously and went away with great satisfaction. I explained to them what was to be done within five hours of death.

As per Roshni's procedure, I wanted to send Mrs Sundari a letter, thanking her for her valuable donation, along with a memento that she could treasure. I also wished to call her over the phone and praise her for fulfilling her husband's wishes.

When I made a call to Mrs Sundari, she accepted my thanks with grief, and in a feeble voice requested me to meet her when I was free. The visit could only take place after a week as she insisted that I should come only when her son was working on a day shift. She explained to me how her husband would keep a piece of cotton below the pillow and remind her every now and then that she should keep moist cotton on both the eyes as soon as death came. This had been going on for a few years. On the day that he died, as she followed the instructions given by him, her son had stopped her. He did not want to donate the eyes; she was helpless. She showed him the pledge forms but her son was adamant.

The eyes had to be removed within six hours and she did not know what to do. Relatives had started coming over to share their grief. One of her close relatives, Lakshmi, asked Mrs Sundari whether the eyes were donated as per her husband's wish. Mrs Sundari told her everything and Lakshmi too tried to convince Mrs Sundari's son, but he told her that if his mother went against his wishes he would not perform the last rites for his father.

Lakshmi declared that she would arrange for everything, including the cremation. She did it! We got two precious eyes which were transplanted to two different patients!

After a month, when we had the next meeting of Roshni, Mrs Sundari's son came to meet people who had been the recipients of eye-donations (not the same who had received the eyes of his father, as we do not disclose the information) and he apologised before the audience for trying to stop his mother from donating the eyes. He also became a member of Roshni and promised to give all the help he could.

Mrs Sundari is very much relieved now as she is confident that her son will fulfil her wish to donate her eyes also on the day of her death.

Vijayalakshmi Ramachandran

The Scooty Ride

People say that I often make them cheerful with my childlike humour, despite my age (I am now slipping into my mid-thirties). Goes without saying, that this makes me feel good. I owe this disposition to a very close friend and a former colleague of mine, Aarti Kapoor Christie, a Delhiite who has now married a Greek–American and lives in New York with her family.

Aarti opened her heart only to me. She has been through several unimaginable traumas in life, yet retained her sanity—and that childlike cheer. Her presence in the office meant a good day for all.

Aarti also taught me to be humble with sellers at red-light intersections. Once, she was going home from office on her Scooty. As she stopped at a red light, a small girl came rushing to her. She was selling flowers that had almost wilted. She requested Aarti, 'Please take these. I'll give you all of them for twenty rupees,' knowing, perhaps, that no one would buy those lifeless flowers. Aarti wouldn't either. Instead, she asked the girl, 'Have you ever ridden a Scooty?' The girl forgot her flowers for a moment. Wide-eyed, she replied, 'No. Never.' Aarti asked her, 'You want to?' Hesitatingly, the girl looked at her. The traffic light turned green. 'Quick!' Aarti encouraged her. 'Sit, quickly!'

Unwilling to let the chance slip away, the girl quickly squeezed her flowers under her small arms and jumped on the backseat. Aarti knew that she was scared too. 'Hold on,' she commanded. Hesitantly, the girl clutched Aarti at her waist with both hands while Aarti swiftly put her flowers in the Scooty's basket. And they zoomed off.

The next red light was at a good distance. On the way, Aarti asked her, 'Are you scared?' 'Not really,' the girl replied. 'Maza aa raha hai (It's fun).'

The cool evening breeze caressed the girl's face, and she stretched both her hands out, as if embracing life. Aarti watched her in the rear-view mirror. When she stopped at the next red light, the girl got down, thanking her with her smiling eyes. She skipped her way back, playing with her ageing flowers.

After she'd narrated this incident to me, Aarti explained, 'I didn't want to just buy those flowers out of charity. It would have sent her a wrong signal. She would have expected others to do the same. But I could definitely make her smile instead.'

Rana Siddiqui Zaman

The Stuffed Toy

The kids waited with bated breath as I disclosed our agenda for the monthly picnic.

'Tell me which state is known for the maximum number of ice cream outlets?' All fifty of them screamed in unison, 'Gujarat!'

'And that's where we will head tomorrow—to the Havmore ice cream factory! We will see how "boring" milk turns into yummy ice cream! And you get to eat as much as you can!'

Their eyes sparkled in anticipation and their mouths watered: most of the fifty underprivileged children in our 'Wednesdays Classroom' programme had never tasted ice cream before. The closest they had come to it was its poor cousin—the one-rupee 'gola' (iced-candy) that they received as a treat from their parents, and that not more than three or four times in the entire year! Milk or milk products to these bright-eyed children was perhaps more exclusive to them as is a fancy Swiss chocolate to our 'privileged' kids!

They were dressed in their best clothes with their hair oiled and neatly combed, small trinkets made of cheap metal hung proudly on their tiny delicate necks. They stood in two perfect files, eyes smiling, and lips breaking into the widest curve at the slightest nudge. I could gather that most had not had much sleep the previous night for they were eagerly awaiting the morning sun to set forth on their fabulous picnic. Just watching their animated faces made our day—the 'our' being my two girls, aged twelve and nine, and I. My daughters had agreed to accompany me on the trip. This was my indirect way of introducing them to a life beyond their own needs and wishes, and of course sending a signal on the virtue of judicious spending. The lesson that was in store for not just them but me as well, was way beyond what I could have expected!

Accompanying us were a few NRI volunteers, students who were on their service vacation to India. One of them was carrying a stuffed bunny which she gave to a small boy of about eight. I saw this little boy, Jignesh, happily playing with his new possession—hugging it, conversing with it, even feeding the bunny from his precious cup of ice cream!

And then, a boy even younger than Jignesh went up to him and asked him if he could hold the bunny for a while. Unhesitatingly, Jignesh passed on his treasured possession to this little chap. For the rest of our trip, the bunny stayed with the little boy; Jignesh participated in all our group activities, though I did see him steal a glance every now and then at his bunny.

I felt sad for the little boy and wondered where this would lead. As our trip came to an end and we were again getting into the bus, I kept close to the two boys. I had made up my mind to get another bunny for the little chap and present it to him at next week's class. I saw the little boy make his way to Jignesh to hand over the bunny to the rightful owner; I saw that his eyes did not have greed for that toy, but pleasure that he could have had those moments with it. I saw that it tore his little heart, yet he knew that the bunny did not belong to him. What values! What self-respect! I marvelled at the integrity of this little boy and was making a mental note to meet up with his family, when I saw Jignesh turn to him and say, 'Tane bahut gamiyu, tu rakhi le (You really loved it, you keep it).'

The little boy jumped with joy and ran away to show his prized possession to the others. My eyes met Jignesh's and he looked away as if embarrassed. Little Jignesh—who I am sure had never owned a toy before—did not even want that his gesture should be noticed!

I turned towards my girls and saw the same expression in their eyes as well, that of deep awe and respect for Jignesh. Their eyes reflected something else too: an understanding of wherein lies true happiness—not in hoarding one gadget after another, but in the joy of sharing. A feeling that can warm up the insides like no material possession can!

I was supposed to be their teacher, well it was I who learnt a precious lesson that day!

Raksha Bharadia

The Volunteer

He was a volunteer just like any of us.

He'd spend about an hour every day, talking to the differently-abled kids. He'd play with them, teach them simple stuff, like how to wash their hands or how to write a capital 'A'. He wasn't that good at connecting with them or anything. Not like some of the other volunteers who were a big hit.

But the thing about this middle-aged, slightly-balding guy, was that he was consistent. He was the chap you could be sure would be there whether a train got derailed en route or the city was flooded beyond belief. He'd come straight from work. Maybe he had a boring banker's job? Or sold insurance? No one knew, and no one ever thought to ask. Every evening, like clockwork, he'd come in at 6 p.m., take off his tie, roll up his shirt sleeves, tuck his beat-up leather pouch under the table and get started with volunteer work without any dilly-dallying.

It was only after his customary hour, when he was pushing the chair back against the wall from where he'd taken it and smoothing back his comb-over, that he'd make eye contact with any of us. He made desultory conversation at this time. 'Really hot today!' he'd say. Or 'Tendulkar's quite in form, isn't he?' Most days, I'd just mumble a vague response or nod my head. I didn't want to encourage him. You never know with these forty-something guys, they always seem on the verge of a mid-life crisis, I used to think.

And so it went on for two years. He was like that Mr Cellophane from the *Chicago* film. There, but kind of invisible. As in most groups, the usual little dramas took place with us as well. There were love stories and hate stories. There were jealousies, there were triumphs. There were moments of uncontrolled happy laughter and there were frustrated tears. But he was oblivious to it all. We admired his commitment, but we wrote him off as sub-human, someone who didn't succumb to the usual frailties. Someone even went to the extent of saying he probably had no emotions!

And then one day, he didn't turn up at his usual time. We assumed that he was ill or away on holiday. But when he didn't show up for a week, and then a whole month, we started to feel his absence. We noticed things we'd conveniently overlooked before. That he didn't do the glamorous stuff like telling stories or handing out the storybooks. But that he'd been quietly doing all the little tasks that we didn't like to do. Like mopping up spills when the kids were careless with their juice. Or going down on his hands and knees to pick up every last crayon after the drawing session was over.

We decided we should try to contact him. I was nominated for the job, not because I was closest to him, but purely because I had the most time on my hands then. I looked up his details in the volunteer book. There was no phone number, just an address. 'Oh no!' I grumbled. 'Now I'll have to go and talk to him in person.'

And so I went. He lived in one of the posh areas of the city. I was impressed by the guard in his building taking down my name and occupation (I didn't say 'student', but rather pompously, 'social worker', so I'd rise in the watchman's esteem). He escorted me to the right doorway and I waited impatiently as the bell twanged an extended instrumental version of *Didi tera dewar deewana*.

The door was opened by a little girl, maybe nine or ten years old. She was adorable, with pixie eyes and delicate features. As she let me in and pranced away, I saw that she wore a frilly cap, pulled snugly around her head, right down to her ears. 'Daddeeeee! Aunty has come to see you . . .' she called down a long corridor.

The man I was seeking emerged, looking rather different in a rumpled kurta-pyjama. I had never seen him with stubble on his chin or rubber flip-flops on his feet, so I was a bit taken aback. But he was even more surprised to see me. Yet he was courteous, offering me tea and indicating a comfortable chair. I sat down awkwardly and decided to get to the point. 'You haven't been coming for a month. I thought . . . we thought . . . we should ask what happened . . .' I blurted out.

He sat back on the sofa, cupped his chin in his palm, cleared his throat. 'Dolly, go inside and put your toys on the shelf,' he said to his little daughter, who was twirling around the bead curtain that hung from the door that led out of the room. She carefully untwirled herself, pouted dramatically, and flounced out of the room in a huff.

Then he turned to me, opening out his hands, palms facing me. 'What can I say, it's difficult to explain,' he started. 'You see Dolly—that's my daughter—suffers from blood cancer. She's been in and out of treatment for a long time now . . .' Stunned, realising the significance of that cap now, I spluttered, 'But . . .' 'Wait, let me finish,' he said, demonstrating an authority I'd never seen in him before. 'We were doing fine until last month. Dolly was even attending school whenever she could. But something else happened. About a month ago, my wife walked out on us. She said she couldn't deal with all the illness and the hospital visits anymore. Unlike me, she hadn't found an outlet for the stress. When I volunteered with all of you, I could be calm, useful. I could get time off from the intensely emotional atmosphere at home. But she had no such release. I understood her feelings. Even so, I did feel abandoned when she walked out. I had to handle that. And I had to be there for my daughter more than ever. I'm still figuring everything out. But I'm confident Dolly and I will be fine. And I'll be back to help the kids soon too,' he smiled.

I was overwhelmed by his courage, his grace under pressure, his unabashed optimism. I tried to smile in support, but it came out like a grotesque grimace. I said something, words of comfort that seemed alarmingly inadequate. Then I made my excuses and literally rushed out of his home.

As I walked away, my mind was in turmoil. I thought how terribly we'd misjudged him. Of course he had emotions, of course he cared. It was just that he was busy dealing with problems that were much larger than we could have ever imagined! When I told the others, we all shared a moment of sombre introspection. And then we all decided to visit him and help him get his life back in order.

After all, he was a volunteer just like any of us.

Priya Pathiyan

Vocal in Times of Beauty

To stand up and speak out against cold injustice, against the blind wrong-doing that we see in the world—that is one kind of activism. But there is another kind. A rarer form of fire-in-the-belly commitment to a much less talked-about cause. Tell me, do you stand up and speak out when you encounter a moment of unexpected joy, warmth, beauty or compassion in your life? Do you stop to say so when you stumble across something that makes you smile—or are you in the habit of registering the remarkable without remark? Are you a bystander of beauty, a mute spectator of special-ness? Do you let the silver-lining moments of the day slide into an insignificant silence, or do you seize them as a chance to make something bloom?

Sometimes I think of all the nice things I've thought about other people and never shared, of the unacknowledged gifts I've received from the world, and the vast clutter of unuttered statements of gratitude and appreciation. A stain of regret tinges the thought of all those unspoken words, un-acted-upon intentions, stacked up like unpaid bills somewhere in the recesses of my mind. 'Be vocal in times of beauty.' I don't fully recall where I first came across that phrase. But I remembered it recently as I was standing near the register at a café where we were holding an event.

I heard a customer tell the woman at the counter, 'I just want to say, it makes such a difference to come in here and find you looking so happy to be doing what you're doing. It makes us want to come in here more often, it really does.' It struck me that here was someone being vocal in a time of beauty. There was a power to the moment that galvanised action. We had a bowl of 'smile stones' inside the café that were meant for the guests at the event. I grabbed a blue one with a particularly wide smile. The woman was putting cream in her coffee. I walked up to her, holding out a smile card and the little stone. 'I want to give you these,' I said. Her face lit up in amazement, 'How did you know I needed a smile?' She looked down again at the little blue stone smiling up at her. 'Thank you,' she said, giving me a hug. I smiled and went back to the café to attend to the rest of the event.

Five minutes later the same woman walked in; there were bright tears in her eyes as she leaned over to hold my hand and whisper to me, 'You really have no idea how much that meant. My mother and I are here from Hawaii to be with my uncle. He's in the hospital after a triple bypass surgery. We've been here four days and it's been really hard. And then you came by with this smile at just the right time. God bless you! Aloha.' And with another swift hug she was gone, throwing a grateful glance over her shoulder as she left.

It dawned on me a little later that my gesture was not so much one of generosity but of gratitude. She was in essence thanking me for thanking her! Funny how sometimes what goes around comes around more swiftly than we might imagine. But all I really want to remember from this story is—to be vocal in times of beauty.

Pavi Mehta

6

A MATTER OF PERSPECTIVE

We need not think alike to love alike.
—David Ferenc

A Carnation by Any Other Name

Here is the church and here is the steeple,
We sure are cute for two ugly people
I don't see what anyone can see,
In anyone else but you ...

Whenever I hear these lines, I can't stop smiling. This should have been my theme-song back in college. College ... where emotions were messy and the mood for the day was dominated by whether you had a glimpse of your crush or not. When anyone asked you if this was love, you would nod vigorously and proclaim that it could hardly be something as ephemeral as an infatuation.

And when your head is in the clouds, you rarely notice your friends ... much less a sweet, unassuming Gujju boy. He liked me and would drop subtle hints. He tried to make me read between the lines, but I was marching to the beat of a different drummer.

We were both painfully shy. As my crush on someone else waned, he mustered up the courage to ask me out: a simple walk at a famous local-spot. What the poor chap wasn't to know, was that I lived slap-bang in the middle of the spot. Coming from a marginally orthodox south-Indian family, I could just imagine the expression on my father's face to see me on a date right under his nose! The grand rendezvous never happened.

His bumbling attempts continued. It was Traditional-Day at college ... a time for us to step out in our finest Indian glad rags. I wore a vibrant sari in tussar-silk and he was flatteringly flustered. There was a flower-vendor at the college gates who was selling a motley bunch consisting of roses, carnations and the odd lily. After much hemming and hawing, my friend blurted out, 'Can I buy you an incarnation?' There was a long pause. His eyes grew wide with horror. Mine grew wide with the effort to control my laughter. And then, just like that, we simultaneously cracked up.

We never ended up together. We stayed friends and gradually even drifted apart. New groups were formed and old friendships faded away. I don't even know where he is today, but he reminds me of an uncomplicated time. A time when romance was in its fledgling-stage, fresh and untouched by the cynicism that colours our present-day relationships.

Namratha Kumar

Appu

When the family first moved into our colony of college teachers, we never suspected there would be anything that would jar our strictly middle-class sensibilities. There was a man, wife, old parents, a dog and a woman of unspecified relationship to the rest.

But then there started the raised voices in the still of the night, followed by the suppressed sobs of a woman, and the dog's bark. We were dismayed, more so when we saw the wife after such skirmishes, sporting a much bruised face as she went about her work the next morning.

By bits and pieces, the puzzle was resolved.

Sirnaik had been a lecturer in a college, sacked from his job for taking classes more often than not in an inebriated condition. The unexplained woman in the house was the proverbial 'other woman'.

The sympathy of the colony people went unconditionally to the wife, Meena Tai, and incidentally to the dog Appu, who was fanatically loyal to her.

Appu was a friendly dog and got along with people very well. My dog Tommy as a rule barked furiously at anyone who as much as glanced at our house, as though he sensed dishonest intentions. Our stock with people at such moments touched a dismal low.

Tommy was a loner. But surprisingly enough, he got along very well with Appu, perhaps because Appu unconditionally accepted Tommy as the leader. He frequented our house and would sit for hours with Tommy.

This made me kind of responsible for Appu's wellbeing, and as Meena Tai was not in a position to, I undertook to finance his visits to the vet for the various periodical shots and the expenses involved in the surgical removal of his recurrent tumours.

So, like P.G. Wodehouse's Ukridge, I came to own half a share in the dog. That is, until a third claimant appeared on the scene.

The kids of the colony got quite fond of the friendly dog. Appu would keep a watchful eye whenever they played on the road. He would be the first person at the scene whenever there was a minor mishap, as if to assess the damage.

That was exactly what happened when Mr Bhagwat's scooter skidded and he fell off the vehicle. It was around three in the afternoon and the road was deserted. Appu, who was lazing on the road, barked wildly and ran to the unfortunate man's side. Someone came out of their house hearing him bark, and the alarm raised by him brought the others.

Bhagwat was helped to his feet and reached his house supported by the people on the road. He was a widower and lived alone in the house next to the Sirnaiks.

Until the incident, Bhagwat had paid scant attention to the Sirnaiks or to Appu. But Appu's barking for assistance, and the old couple's and Meena Tai's kind concern over the mishap thawed Bhagwat's attitude towards the neighbours. Thus began a camaraderie between Bhagwat and the old Sirnaiks and Meena Tai. Appu played the hero's role quite ably, following Bhagwat wherever he went, like the legendary Mary's lamb. Perhaps he was hankering after a master and Mr Bhagwat stepped into the role with ease.

The lonely man and the dog grew very close to each other. Appu was an inseparable companion when Bhagwat went on his early-morning walks.

One morning, Bhagwat took a new route for his walk and Appu decided that he did not like it. After every few feet, he would run ahead and fall in front of him and whine piteously, begging Bhagwat not to go ahead. Bhagwat got thoroughly exasperated and turned back home, followed by a jubilant Appu.

To his shock, he found the door of his house ajar and a burglar busy collecting his booty. Bolting the door from outside, Bhagwat raised an alarm. The thief was caught and handed over to the police.

Appu became a hero once again, not just to Bhagwat, but to the entire colony. He was now credited with ESP!

But as one who has cared for any number of dogs, and knows their ways well, I had a simple explanation for Appu's odd behaviour. Whenever a dog enters a new territory, he is taken to task by the resident dogs of the area. Appu wanted to avoid any unpleasantness and insisted on their return, and the unfortunate thief just happened to choose that day to break into Bhagwat's house.

But Appu was basking in his new-found glory and I did not want to disabuse people of their opinion about his supposed ESP capabilities!

One morning, there was quite a bit of commotion at Sirnaik's place. The old couple was standing at the gate looking lost and Mr Sarnaik was talking loudly to his mistress who was replying in kind.

Apparently, Meena Tai had disappeared. People's sympathies were fully with her—till it was found that Bhagwat had left as well.

My husband very casually told me, 'On the night of Meena Tai's disappearance, around two in the morning, when I got up for a glass of water, I stood at the window for a few moments. I just saw Appu jumping into a car and the car moving away.'

In a month's time, the sensation died down and we all reverted to our dull routine.

All this would have faded from memory had I not accidentally met Bhagwat a year after, in a town where I had been to attend a meeting.

He greeted me very cheerfully. 'Meena and I very often remember your kindness to Appu,' he told me. 'I am sure our disappearance caused quite a bit of talk. You see, I decided to return to my native place where I have landed property. I wanted to take Appu with me.'

I said, 'But why did you have to take Meena Tai? No one knew that there was anything going on between you.'

'There was nothing going on between us. I persuaded her to come with me because Appu is very attached to her. I did not want him to be unhappy.'

Have you ever heard of a more valid reason for a man eloping with a middle-aged housewife?!

Revathi Seshadri

It Happens Only in India

It was way back in 1986, soon after my family moved to Kolkata from Delhi. We had to attend a wedding in Chennai on August 24. The groom was my mother's favourite nephew, and there was no way she was going to miss it. My school refused to give me two weeks' leave since I was a new student, so instead of two weeks, we decided to take just a week off. We would leave on August 16, Saturday, and reach Chennai on August 17, with plenty of time before the wedding. My father, who had to go to Delhi on work, would join us only on the day of the wedding.

On August 9, I fell sick with high fever and vomiting. Every day, my mother battled to keep my temperature low. There was no question of not going to the wedding.

On August 16, a misguided driver wasted time trying to get me an Avomin. We got stuck in a traffic jam on Howrah Bridge, and how the Ambassador we were in managed to reach the station on time is a mystery my mother and I can never solve. The train was just starting to move, but the driver asked us to run and get into any compartment we could. He threw our heavy trunk in after us.

My mother then made me wait in a ladies coupe and went looking for our seat. Thank god for the vestibules. In our allotted coupe, she found two young women of around twenty-five, waiting eagerly for her. This was their first journey alone; they were returning home after visiting an aunt in Kolkata, and the aunt had been anxious to meet my mother and hand over charge.

We shifted to our seats in Kharagpur. Since I had not been keeping well, my mother had packed a few chapathis and some pickle for herself. Since nothing was staying in my stomach in any case, where was the need to pack anything for me? But as luck would have it, that night I had some jhal muri from a vendor in the train, threw up everything, and then felt perfectly fine (should I have done this earlier?), and hungry. No worries, the young ladies told us. They had bread.

So, as it can happen only in train journeys, quick friendship was formed with the two ladies and we looked forward to the next few hours spent in pleasant company.

Then came Rajahmundri. It was early morning, and by evening, we would be in Chennai. But it seemed like we were spending six hours in Rajahmundri itself! The driver of a Howrah Mail that came from Chennai warned the driver of our train that the Godavari river had swelled following torrential rains, and that he had barely managed to cross the bridge. He asked us not to venture that way. So an engine was sent to test and the verdict passed was that we would have to avoid the bridge.

We retraced our route back as our destination now was Raipur. En route we saw Vijayanagaram for the second time. We slept, assuming that we would find ourselves at Raipur in the morning. But what wonder, we were again backtracking and found ourselves in Vijayanagaram yet again, as a goods train had derailed en route! That night, the train was back in Kharagpur, just two hours away from Howrah! We were stopped at every signal since all scheduled trains got priority over us. At every station we touched, canteens were empty since our train was not expected. How did we manage? I don't know, and yet, we were never hungry, never weary, never upset.

So now, we went all the way to Nagpur. At some point, a typical rowdy got on the train. Since ours was the first coupe, and he would always be near the door, we kept the door shut because the two ladies might have found it uncomfortable (I was only thirteen then).

How we misjudge people. He used his brawn-power to get us food at the stations. And at one point, he bought the entire compartment ice-cream! People from other compartments complained that, because of him, they were not getting anything to eat! This was not the first time a train had been detoured, for him, and he told us tales of how they survived earlier—by getting flour from villages on the way. After that, we were less wary of him.

We finally reached Chennai on August 20. Unfortunately, the Coromandals that started after us had already taken the alternative route, learning from our experience. And so the ones that started on 17th and 18th reached before we did—and the announcers never bothered to say which one was expected. So our people at Chennai had to visit the station every day to check on us. With no cell phones in those days, they must indeed have wondered at our fate and had the worst fears about our fate. My father in Delhi was even more cut-off, since communication over landline was also practically nil because of the rains.

But for those of us who were on the train, it was unmitigated fun. We were on water most of the time; because of the monsoons, the tracks were all submerged. We joked it was a teertha yatra. We noted down station names and figured out that we had touched six instead of the original three. There were music sessions, card sessions. We exchanged anecdotes. There was a man from Kerala who had us in splits. We even planned a concert on the train, since my mother and the two girls could sing. Though that didn't materialise, the details kept us busy.

And, most importantly, we bonded. The bonds may not have lasted, but for those five days on the train, it was as if we were with friends.

Tell me, where else can such a thing happen?

S. Meera

Lost in London

This story is a thank you to the nameless Iranian student who helped me in my hour of need, selflessly. Thanks a lot, buddy. There comes a time when you least expect it, that God reaffirms your faith in humanity; this was one of those days. But let me start at the beginning.

I can never forget Monday, 24 September 2001. My wife and son got lost in London on Oxford Street, which is like Nariman Point in Mumbai in the evening: horribly crowded and choc-a-bloc with commercial and shopping establishments.

We had gone to London to meet a doctor for my elder son, who suffers from a genetic disorder. The doctor's appointment at the hospital was on the 25th, and we wanted to make a practice-run the day before, so that on the day of the appointment, we would not be late.

Why a practice-run? Because the route was complicated, needing several changes of transport. We reached the hospital uneventfully, and decided to go shopping from there to Selfridges.

As we started walking towards the shop, we realised that it was farther than we had thought, and since we had both our children with us, the going was slow. We decided to head back home. I wanted to try an alternate route from a station that was closer to where we were. I took out my map and asked someone if we had a choice. Hrithik, my younger son, was in the pram with me and Darshan was with my wife Deepali. He disliked walking, so Deepali was carrying him on her shoulders. By the time I'd taken directions, inexplicably, I lost sight of Deepali. I panicked but willed myself to stay calm. Just then I caught sight of Deepali's purse in the pram. This meant she neither had any money on her, nor the address or the telephone number of the place we were staying in. I didn't know what to do. I told myself that Deepali would be there any moment, tracing back her steps, searching for me. But though I tried to be calm, I was panicking. I frantically ran ahead, but saw no sign of her; I returned to where we'd been and still no sign of her. I did this four to five times but could not locate Deepali. The time now was 6 p.m. and it was getting dark; it had been a full hour since I'd last seen Deepali and Darshan. I had to face the inevitable: Deepali and Darshan were lost in London. To top it, I spotted the evening *Sun* newspaper headlines: 'Tourist found murdered in Thames river'. Dark thoughts started entering my mind.

I called my wife's cousins, with whom we were staying, and told them that Deepali was lost. They asked me to call the police immediately from the nearest store. I was literally shivering and calling up the police in an alien land was the farthest thing from my mind. But I did just that.

Seeing the state I was in, a stranger, an Iranian student, approached me and asked me what had happened. I narrated the whole story and told him that my wife did not even have her passport or any money. I even showed him my wife's photograph. My last bet was that maybe she had walked all the way to Holborn station from where we were supposed to catch the train for our return journey. But the station was a distance away, and since she was carrying Darshan on her shoulders, I didn't think it would be possible for her to reach there. It was my last hope, though. He told me not to worry and that we would find her. He stood with me for ten minutes, but still there was no sign of Deepali. Suddenly I saw him leave, and I thought that was but natural. Why would he waste his time with a total stranger?

Unbeknownst to me, he had taken his bike to go to Holborn station. There he met a woman outside the station with a child on her shoulders. He asked her whether she was Deepali. My wife was shocked and surprised. He asked her whether she was lost, to which she told him that it was her husband who was lost! I suppose even under stress, her sense of humour had not deserted her. Then the stranger bought a bottle of Evian water and a bar of chocolate for my son. He informed her that I was looking for her and was waiting nearby and that I would be with her shortly.

The stranger came back to inform me that my wife was waiting nearby Holborn station. The police too arrived just then, and helped me reach the station. I wept tears of joy on finding my wife there. Even she was surprised that I was getting down from a police car. And in the entire melee, the stranger vanished without even giving us time to thank him properly!

Ameet Surana

My Hero

I was driving home after work one day. The route I take is along the banks of the river Gomti, that flows through Lucknow, then over a bridge to what is called the trans-Gomti area.

I am a cautious driver, and as always, when I came to the sharp turn from the 'bandha' road to the main road, I slowed down, to find that a rickshaw was parked at the curve. Cursing under my breath I turned just a little to the right, unaware that a large black Tata Sumo was racing up the main road. When I did see it, it was already too late. The big car hit my little Maruti 800 on the side, smashing the headlight and ripping off the front fender completely. In fact, I saw it whizzing ahead, with my fender stuck to its side. Then it gave a little jerk, my car's fender fell on the road and the big car raced away!

I was shaken but somehow managed to park my car by the side of the road. Suddenly a little urchin turned up. He picked up my fender, which thankfully hadn't suffered much damage, helped me to put it on the rear seat and gave me a little lecture on safe driving. I let him in next to the driver's seat and we drove ahead to a more open space to assess the damage.

The car was driving fine so I guessed everything else was

in order. Just then a school bus crossed us and little heads appeared at the windows, laughing at the pathetic state of my car. That relieved the tension. My helper and I had a hearty laugh too. Then we stopped an ice-cream vendor who happened to be going by just then. I treated my 'hero' to a large cone, made him promise me that he would always remain the sweet, helpful boy that he was, and drove off to my service workshop!

Rehana Ali

Of Dal-Chawal and Biryani

'You are my dal-chawal man,' I told him. And he said in exasperation, *'What?'* I looked at him and said, nonchalantly, 'Of course, you are.' Being an East Indian, I have been brought up on a staple diet of dal-chawal. You might not believe it, but my maternal grandmother died at the age of ninety-five without ever tasting a chapati. In her world, it's rice that rocked. I'm sure that this was the reason she wanted me to marry somebody from Kalikata (she did not say Calcutta, or Kolkata, like the rest of us), since I wasn't interested in marrying anybody from Orissa. She thought a plate of rice would make my marriage work. She didn't have a very high opinion of people who had roti and sabzi (she thought perhaps they were stingy people who did not want to spend money on food).

Anyway, let me move away from my granny, who I presume must be having a good time in heaven, and return to my dal-chawal-man funda. I have four dal-chawal men in my life (two of whom don't live in the same city as I do), and a biryani man. My dal-chawal men are very much like my comfort food. There are no ego issues involved with them. There are days when one of them calls me seven–eight times. Some calls can go on for thirty minutes interspersed with a minimum of twenty 'bye, take care's. There are times when

I call one of them desperately, in the middle of the day, when I have my once-in-a-blue moon sweet craving. They are there to discuss crazy colleagues, naughty nieces, art, architecture, relationships, porn films and size zero. And we all know a lot about each other's families too, though I have not met them. So if a Nagpur didi's daughter is having a problem in her career, then I am asked my expert opinion. When I'm distressed about my mom's failing health, I go to one of them and cry my heart out. And after a glass of vodka or kadak masala chai, I'm ready to conquer the world.

It's not that we don't fight. We can argue endlessly on the relevance of a particular painting or a Bollywood flick. Till now, though, we haven't banged down the phone or the door shut after one of those volatile arguments. And the next day, when the call comes, asking 'Hi, let's go to dinner tonight', then it's as if the argument never happened. That's the power of dal-chawal. It's a part of me. It comes to me naturally, without having to make any conscious effort.

Well, the story of biryani is a tad different. It's a little bit distant. Not easily available. I had my first taste of biryani when I was eleven. It was at Alfa (or Alpha) restaurant in Secunderabad. The restaurant had dazzling interiors with pieces of coloured glass on the wall. I fell in love with biryani the very first time I tasted it. One mouthful of it, and I thought, 'This could be heaven'. I have never felt the same intense way with another dish since. Food is a passion with me, and when it comes to biryani, it's pure love. At the same time, I can't live without my dal-chawal.

But then biryani being biryani, you can't have it every day. You can't get too close to it. The same goes with my biryani man. There's a sense of distance and a sense of aloofness. My dal-chawal man is my 3 a.m. call. The one I complain to about my cell phone not behaving well. The one I share my happiness with when I hear my niece playing the piano over the phone from faraway Atlanta. These are not the things I share with my biryani man. He's my aspiration. He's my desire. He's my passion. He's my love. He's my luxury in a world filled with mundane necessities. He's the one who takes me away from a world full of worries about 'dal-chawal'. Like the succulent biryani, he's the richness in my life; the person that makes me feel like a millionaire at the end of the day without owning a house, a car, a diamond—not even an LCD television. He's the billboard weaving a million dreams in the neon-lit streets of the city I live in. He's the wave in the golden sea of Puri, which stops just in front of my feet when I so want it to come and embrace me with a tingling feeling. But then there's a beauty in falling waves—why must we always revel in rising waves?

At the end of the day, what's there on my dinner plate? Dal-chawal. But I live another day in the hope of that mouthful of biryani. And every night before I sleep, I say a prayer: if the next meal is going to be my last meal, then let it be biryani. What's life without desire?

Akanksha

On the Birth of My Nephew

Ah! Little fellow,
Welcome to the arms,
Of a proud uncle.

Welcome into this world of ours.
We have many things for you.
You shall have them
As a young man.

Books,
Dogma,
Music.

Guns,
And roses.
Especially roses.

Tell me, nephew,
(Though I know you cannot tell)
What will the world be like,
In your time?

Will there still be roses,
And the time and tenderness,
To give them to pretty girls?

A MATTER OF PERSPECTIVE

Will the child's laugh,
The sparrow's twitter
And the sunrise on the sea
Still be beautiful?

Will all men,
Who the wise say
Are born equal,
Will they die equal
And happy?

Or would steel
Still shed blood?

Will the madness that has been
The fate of all mankind,
The plunder and plague,

Still abound?

I hope there will be roses,
And the beauty of love

Still prevail in the end.

Nephew (how you sleep!)
Someday you will be

The father, and I the son
And you will lead me by
The hands that hold you now,
Into a future unseen.

Raamesh Gowri Raghavan

Still Indian After Two Hundred Years, Two Oceans, Three Continents and Thousands of Miles of Separation

'You look Indian!' she exclaimed in surprise, as I shared a basin with her, washing our hands clean before our meal. My worn salwar-kameez and rich brown skin had deceived this IRMA student up until I opened my mouth and revealed my American tongue. I did not realise how good it made me feel. I had succeeded in tricking a native desi into believing that I was one of her own kind. I marvelled at how, in America, being mistaken for an Indian, an FOB ('Fresh Off the Boat' Indian), would have probably been seen as an insult. Now it was the biggest compliment I could have ever received.

I did not ever think, even in my wildest dreams, that I would be here in India. Nor probably did my great grandparents, who boarded a British boat off to the uncertain land of Guyana back in 1838. I wonder why they left in the first place. Were they tired of the dusty, crowded streets, of dodging camels, street vendors, and cow dung? Were they hungry for something new and different—some white gold, British-promised land, with some sweet plantains on the side? Or were they simply poor, thirsty, and walking barefoot for miles to the shore where a ship awaited to give them something more hopeful than begging for a few paisa? I wonder why they did not return to India after their five years of indentured servitude. Did they learn to love the Amazon rainforest and manatees swimming in black waters? Did they not miss the food and the culture and the chaos? Or did they simply fear the same things that I did? That they were no longer Indian enough to return. That living across the ocean had washed away their essence. A white wolf dressed in brown sheep skin.

Over the past few months, I have sung the Indian national anthem countless number of times. As an American, I cannot help but become a little nostalgic for the country of my birth. After singing *Jana Gana Mana* for the twelfth time, I made the careless comment of telling one of the children, with whom I worked, that I missed 'my country'. Without a moment of hesitation he replied in surprise: 'Isn't this your country?'

India. Is India my country? After nearly two hundred years, two oceans, three continents and thousands of miles of separation from this country, is it still mine? Can one claim a nationality, a civilisation, a culture? Does a tree say it belongs to the seed from which it has sprung?

After being welcomed with open arms into the houses of strangers, after being fed ladoos from the hands of widowed older women from Ramapir NoTekro, after being thrown head first into a Gujarati Navratri garba, I have learned that in India, there is no question about the idea of belonging. Belonging is a given. The people of India come from all walks of culture, religion, and life. The essence that is inside of me is the same as that in the initial seeds of India that were planted in the fertile soil of Guyana. A child still belongs to her mother no matter how old she has grown, how far she has travelled, or how long a time she has spent separated from her care. After a few months, I have learned that I am still a child of India, and that my mother still recognises me as her own.

'You look Indian!' she exclaimed in surprise, as I shared a basin with her, washing our hands clean before our meal. I dried my hands and smiled at her and replied: 'I am Indian.'

Shivana Naidoo

The Green Salwar Kameez, Bindi and Bangles

On the afternoon of 8 March 2008, my mobile rang. 'Are you Miss Janki Vyas? I am Farhat from Karachi. Do you remember me?' Hearing those words filled me with a wave of nostalgia.

Back in 1986, when I was eighteen and travelling to the US in the Pan American airlines, our aircraft got hijacked in Karachi. We were close to death for fifteen hours, stranded at Karachi airport at the mercy of four merciless terrorists. They opened fire, killing twenty-one passengers and injuring many more. After that nightmarish experience, I was taken to Jinnah Hospital for the bullet and hand grenade injuries I'd sustained on both my legs. I was there for thirty-six hours till a chartered flight came from India to take the passengers back home.

My experiences with the citizens of Karachi was overwhelming and amongst them stands out two resident student doctors I met, one of whom was Farhat. They attended to me in my toughest hour with utmost warmth, expressing their love for India and Indians. They portrayed the best face of humanity at the time I needed it most, at a place I expected it least.

That had been twenty-two years ago. Contacts had faded, numbers lost and we were out of touch. The phone call from Dr Farhat made me realise that memories, however, were still intact.

I remembered how, in the middle of the night, after seeing the face of terror so close to me, I was transferred from the casualty ward to the general one. I was still under searing pain and had no one to talk to, no shoulder to cry on. I could not see a single familiar face around me. I was in a state of deep shock and fear.

Dr Farhat not only nursed my physical wounds, but gave me much-needed emotional succour at that point. My salwar was soaked with blood and, because my leg had swollen, needed to be cut, which he did without any apprehension. Sensing my distressed state, he sat by my side and made conversation through the night and by degrees helped me relax. By the time dawn approached, I did not feel alone anymore.

He excused himself for a few minutes and returned with hot coffee, a toothbrush, a toothpaste, his girlfriend's green salwar-kameez and matching bangles and a bindi! I was overwhelmed!

Farhat then spoke about his girlfriend, and I told him of my fiancé. He asked me about India, Delhi, Indian music and movies; we gossiped about Bollywood stars. I told him about my fascination with Pakistani serials, we found out that we shared a favourite actor—Zoya Ali Khan, the heroine of *Ankahi*, a Pakistani serial. He said India and Pakistan were always one, so naturally we would like and understand each other's culture and people!

Sometime around noon, someone came shouting my name, saying that there was a phone call for me from India. My heart missed a beat! I wanted to fly and take that call, but I could not walk because of my injuries. There were no cordless phones at that time. The man said he would pass on the message that I was recovering. Tears ran down my face as I nodded helplessly. Without saying a word, Dr Farhat, along with the other doctor, Mehboob, lifted me effortlessly and carried me all the way down the hall to the telephone cubicle. I spoke to my family back home and told them that they should not worry as I was in most able and caring hands. That moment was precious to my family, as for them to hear my voice was the only proof of my being alive! That moment was gifted to us by that sensitised soul, who had not even known of my existence a couple of hours ago!

And so we spoke after twenty-four long years, crying and laughing at the same time. He told me about his wife and kids, I told him of my husband and family. And yes, I still have the green salwar kameez, the bindi and the bangles.

Janki Vasant

The Oil Canvas

As a child, I was not really interested in art or painting. I only knew of a few famous artists like Michelangelo, Rembrandt and, of course, M.F. Husain. As a grown-up, too, I could not understand the fuss behind paintings and why one would pay an enormous amount for a six-inch by six-inch frame. Of course, I never owned an art piece.

When I was forty, my dream home was getting constructed. Friends suggested that I liven up the walls with a few works of art. I began visiting galleries and one day found myself at the workshop of a local, world-famous weaver and painter, Rajan.

When I reached his place, I saw him standing under a tree, busy on a huge canvas. The way his frail hand guided the tiny brush over the rather huge canvas seemed to me art in itself, and I stood there transfixed, watching him from a quiet corner. The painting had delicate as well as heavy strokes of warm passionate colours—yellow, red, orange, maroon.

Rajan, realising my presence, stopped his work and welcomed me. I introduced myself and told him that I was interested in his work.

Just then it began to drizzle. We were standing in the open chowk and, worried that the work would get spoilt, I offered to help him carry it inside.

He answered, 'There is no place inside for another canvas. It is already overflowing with my work. If this gets spoilt, I will redo it.' He said this with a tinge of sadness.

He could not have even covered it with a plastic sheet since the paint was wet and would have smudged.

We went into his small studio and he began showing me his work. Meanwhile, the rain outside grew heavy. He excused himself and went to check on the state of his latest 'baby'.

I heard a shout from him, 'Neelam, come out and see this!' I rushed out to the most splendid sight of my life ever.

The rain had textured the canvas. The wet oil paint along with rain drops had trickled down and stood at random intervals in the canvas in a dazzling array of hues—maroon with a small blob of orange at the end; yellow interspersed with red; maroon, red, yellow, orange all crisscrossing each other in a mad riot!

'Ah,' Rajan said, 'it seems the rain god himself wanted to put the finishing touches to my painting!'

And indeed it seemed a joint work of man and Almighty! This happened years ago, but even now, when I think of the painting, it sends goose pimples all over my body! I thought that I saw eternity in that moment. And yes, though my house is done and all its walls adorned, I still visit art galleries. It is this newfound love for art.

Neelam Kothari

Underestimating John

He could neither speak nor understand a word of Hindi or Gujarati. The kids at the slum could barely comprehend a few words of English, and that in a pronounced Indian–English enunciation; his American accent stood no chance with them whatsoever. Yet he was there to 'interact' with the thirty-odd girls at the tekra we teach English to, every Friday.

After completing our agenda for the day, we invited John to take the stage and do his bit. The girls giggled at his white skin and queer dressing (he was in Bermuda shorts and a faded t-shirt), and we looked at him, wondering how on earth he would get past a 'Hi' and 'Namsate!'

Seems there was a lot of learning for us that day!

John gestured to them to form a circle and then stood at its centre. He said 'one' and then placed his left foot a step back and on his toes. He stood silently till all the girls stood in the same position. He said 'two' and dragged his right foot and brought it level with the left one and waited again. The girls said 'two' and followed suit. He said 'three' and shifted his weight from the right to the left. Now his right foot was on its toes while the left foot was flat on the ground. The girls all helped each other do exactly the same. He said 'four' and this time slid the right foot flat back. The girls amidst huge giggles and excitement did it. The ones who were a little confused sought help from the ones who had got it right the first time. In just a few seconds the entire circle was in a disarray with random 'one', 'two', 'three', 'four' coming from all sides. John patiently moved from one girl to another and did his set with them over and over again. We just stood watching, open-mouthed! We had been visiting the girls since the past one year, and even our treats of cake had not caused the laughter and smiles that we now saw on their faces!

And then we heard John scream, 'Together girls!' I am sure they did not know the meaning of 'together', yet within a few seconds they were again standing in a circle in absolute silence. As John counted his numbers from one to four, all thirty moonwalked from the centre of the room to the edges of the wall in a neat circle! The moment they hit the wall John would scream 'Again!' and they would arrange themselves in starting position and slide and swing to his counts once more.

They did ten rounds, twenty ... fifty, till it was time for us to leave!

As we bid our byes, John was on salsa!

Language is important, but there are other ways of communicating!

Anu Chopra

What Is Bigger, Destiny or Karma?

An author, let's call her Aarti, sent in her submission for *Chicken Soup for the Indian Soul* within the approved deadline, but perhaps just a day or two before the last date. By then I had already selected, edited and finalised my 101 stories to be featured in the title. Along with hers, there were about fifty stories that remained unread because I already had my 101 stories. I bundled them all into a folder titled 'Later', and got on with my next project.

Aarti sent me three mails, requesting me to go through her work just once. I replied that I was through with my selection for the title and would look at the submissions later when we began work on the second volume of the title. She replied, 'I know you are pressed for time, but my story will not take more than five minutes. I don't care if you reject it outright, but I do request you to give it just one read. It is about my life and a lesson that I learnt.'

Such a sweet and sincere mail ... I promised her a read the next day. I could not. She waited patiently and wrote to me again a few days later, gently reminding me of her story. I gave her a fresh date and shamelessly procrastinated again. Though it was on my mind that I had to read her work, something always came up that seemed more important. After about a month of repeated reminders, a mail came with the subject: 'Making a writer wait is like cruelty to animals'. Nothing inside the mail—just that line from her. I opened her story right away. It was one of the best I had read so far, truly deserving to be in the *Chicken Soup for the Indian Soul*!

I mailed her with my feedback and apologised that such a powerful, well-written story would not be in the debut compilation, promising her a space in the next title. I felt terribly guilty though, and so I sent the story to my publishing house, marking it as urgent. My publishing house too found the work very good and we decided to take out one of the three stories we were carrying from one author and put Aarti's story instead.

I know appearing in a Chicken Soup title is not a make or break incident for Aarti or anyone—but, for me, this was a lesson in going all out for what one wants. I still marvel at Aarti's persistence; the quiet dignity with which she perhaps changed what might have been—for I have not yet got down to reading the other forty-nine files in the 'Later' folder! For them destiny proved stronger—for Aarti, her karma did!

Raksha Bharadia

Wrong Side of Thirty-Five!

Hits you first when the jokes are no longer on weight or appearances, they are surely and categorically directed towards your age. And to add to this, are the company executive health check-ups that are organised for us 'older' lots. After all, they want to make sure it's a healthy horse they're betting on. Don't want to leave anything to chance. 'Discrimination!' I would love to scream out, but won't I just be playing to the gallery to everyone's delight?

Anyway, the mail regarding my executive health check-up had been sitting in my Inbox for quite some time now. On the one hand, it was a good deal, completely paid for by the company and I would know I was healthy; but on the other, it was as if I was succumbing to the inevitable, 'You're on the wrong side of thirty-five! Need to know all's well with you!'

After the mental tussle, I finally fixed the appointment for a Friday morning. Since it was a company initiative, we were allowed to go on company time—imagine a Friday morning official off!

Tests commenced: a fasting blood sample, then a non-fasting one after two hours of an extremely sweet glucose drink. But where's the breakfast? The email said breakfast would be provided! This measly sweet glass of glucose is breakfast? 'Relax, your BP is rising, breakfast will be provided after all the tests,' I was reassured. So here goes, from PMT to TMT. I was literally exposed to all kind of rays and machines that I probably have never had the chance to see in these thirty-five years of existence, which had me worried. Will this exposure cause more harm than good? There was the ECG, the Echo (pretty freaky with all the wires and clamps on your hands and feet, reminds you of the movie scenes, when the protagonist is declared mentally unstable and is being given shock treatment), chest X-rays, lung function tests, the mammography and the ultrasound's all done. Finally, the general physician and gynaecologist's check-up is due. The obvious questions with the gynaecologist: 'Married?'

'Divorced,' I say, as matter-of-factly as I can. Hold your breath for the next one—'Sexual activity?' 'No,' I say, now almost wincing! After a moment, in an attempt to regain my pride, I add, 'As much as I would like to, but *no*.'

A wry smile and on with the poking business, quite literally.

Here's hoping all the test results are okay at the review session. Till then, I hope to stay healthy and well, *active*!

By the way, did you know racehorses that can't compete any more are shot dead to rest in peace?

Suparnaa Chadda

7
THE SPIRIT LIVES ON

Wake at dawn with a winged heart and give thanks for another day of loving.

–Kahlil Gibran

Daddy Comes Home

It was Sharat Purnima—the full moon of the divine goddess, Kali. We had been dancing five-rhythms for over three hours. What a dance! Over the past two weeks, it had been goddess dances all over the valley, to celebrate Durga, Kali, Shakti, Jagadamba—the feminine principle in all of us. And last night, with the early morning eclipse and the full moon, we saw Kali in her full-blooded glory. It marked the deconstruction of Mother Nature. The monsoon harvest—kharif. The beginning of autumn, falling leaves. A reminder that spring would follow in six short months. With this backdrop, I went home. It was quite late, so I dozed off pretty quickly.

Early morning, as the sun rose, I heard the knocking of a hammer in the newly-built family room. With the recent remodelling, our 'bright room' as we call it, is used sparingly at night, until the kids get up. So I was surprised to hear the knocking. I wondered if it was our contractor—but the construction was pretty much done. Perhaps he had just got into the habit of doing something in our bright room. So I went a-peeping, cautiously.

Lo and behold, it was Daddy! He had always wanted to visit my home but never got a chance to do so, because Mom was always a bit sick. He didn't want to leave her alone and travel the seven seas. So he never got a chance to be with us in California.

That is, until now! But ... something was wrong. Dad was in his usual shorts, going rat-a-tat-a-tat, hammering away. Next to him was a pile of ironed clothes, neatly folded. The iron was still steaming, having been well used. And dad was concentrating fully on the task at hand. On one hand, I was glad that he was here at last. One the other, I had no recollection of picking him up at the airport! That didn't make sense. Perhaps my kid brother, who lives nearby, had picked him up and dropped him here. But he didn't have the keys to the place!

'Dad, you are not supposed to be here!' I exclaimed.

'Why not? Didn't you want me to visit your home, all those years?' he asked.

'Yes, but ... it has been exactly three full years since you passed away! Look, there is even a photograph of you here, days before you died. You can't come here now! Please go back to where you now belong.'

'Well, I would. That is, if you paid any heed to what I always said. Why, look at all these clothes. They've been here for almost a week! You've been waiting for someone else to iron them, huh? And this shelf over here? How long will you curse the carpenter and the cabinetmaker? Didn't I say, it is fun to do things with you own hands?'

'I will. I will. But, please go back to your new home, wherever it is,' I said, my urgency showing in each syllable.

'Okay. But remember to call your mom. She is very much alive!'

He was still there, smiling. Playing with his fake upper incisor, like he always did. All I could do was sprint as fast as I could to my master bedroom, jump into bed, covering myself from head to toe. With a thud, I awoke.

Dad was speaking the truth all right. The whole truth. I

have been wide-awake since. It has been three full years since Guru (as we loving shortened dad's name, Gurudas) left us. He has been lurking in my consciousness ever so often. At times, he pulls these nuggets out of my shadow, and gently taps at the door to my heart.

Shankar Hemmady

Fighting for Karuna's Dignity

The last Board paper was about to begin and Karuna had still not reached the examination hall. *These kids!* I thought. *No responsibility whatsoever.* I waited for another five minutes, then dialled her number on my mobile. A woman answered.

'Karuna hasn't reached school and her paper's about to begin,' I said.

'Sorry! Karuna died this morning.' The answer was like a bolt of lightning.

'Wh ... what!' I had to lean against the table in the veranda to keep from collapsing. 'How?'

'She suddenly took ill. We rushed her to the doctor. She collapsed and didn't recover.'

Click. The line went dead.

I took a deep breath then peeped into the hall. Forty heads turned to me. I could see anxiety writ large on many faces.

'Children, Karuna is ill. She won't be giving her exam,' I said, trying to sound casual. 'Don't worry. We'll inform the Council. They'll do something. You do your paper now.'

The visiting examiner came up to me and drew me out to the veranda.

'You're as white as a sheet,' she said kindly. 'Is everything all right?'

I told her what had happened. She turned pale.

'I'll come back when the paper is over and tell her friends,' I managed to say, and then walked down to my office. Perhaps I had heard wrong. My fingers trembled as I dialled her number again.

'Yes?' another voice.

'I'm Karuna's teacher,' the words came out as a whisper.

'Ma'am, I'm her sister. She died this morning. We have brought her body home from the hospital and the cremation will be held within an hour,' her voice broke.

I had my answer.

If she had been too ill to give the paper, they would surely have informed the school days ago. I saw her face, sweet, gentle and soft. A shy smile. Thick hair, not always neat, framing her face and large expressive eyes.

'Karuna, you're late again. Now stand outside for five minutes.'

'Ma'am ... sorry.' You couldn't not forgive such a child. She looked so ... so vulnerable.

I sat under the neem tree, not knowing what to do next. Poor little girl. What unbearable pressures was she burdened with? At what point in an innocent child's life does reason snap and give way to hopelessness. And why? Why can't adults see a child's desperation behind her giggles and carefree behaviour? Three hours passed. I walked back to the hall.

'May I speak to the children?'

'Yes,' said the visiting examiner softly, pressing my hand.

'Children, Karuna took ill, she was rushed to the hospital. They tried but she didn't recover and passed away ... we'll have a service for her ...'

I couldn't go on. I saw faces shattering like fragile mirrors. I heard the gasps of disbelief. I saw them rise and rush into each other's arms for support, clinging to friends to be able to absorb this terrible truth.

I heard the sobs. I turned away and hid my face in my hands, feeling the hot tears in my palms.

No questions were asked. We just knew the answers, but every child in the hall was united in preserving and protecting their friend's dignity. With a maturity far beyond their years, they wiped one another's tears, promising one another that they would be strong.

Karuna had left no messages except a scrap of paper that said, 'I would like to donate my eyes so that two unseeing persons will have their sight restored. Thank you.'

(You'll be happy to know that two blind persons have received the cornea transplant and now see the world through Karuna's eyes.)

Rehana Ali

Five Airline Toffees

It was always five airline toffees. Every time he travelled, my father would bring me five toffees—never four, never six, always five. There may have been a significance to that number, but I suspect that, like most traditions, it just happened.

Sometimes he'd come back from trips loaded with gifts—sweets from the best confectioner in town, pretty cardigans, pearl necklaces, books and toys; sometimes, he would just not have found the time to shop. But he never came home without those five airline toffees.

I started working around the same time he retired, and the tradition was reversed. Now, I was the one who'd bring five airline toffees every time I came to visit, and he was the one who'd gleefully polish them off in one sitting.

Parkinson's started claiming his body, and dementia his mind, but his sweet tooth remained his own. The last few times I visited him, he barely recognised me. But when he saw the toffees, he proudly said, 'My daughter gets me these toffees too.'

Then, one day, I was on a plane winging homewards. I'd just got the news that my father's heart had finally given up. There was regret (that I missed seeing him by just four days), remorse (that I would never again watch him watching my son throw a ball at him), relief (that he'd finally shed the body and mind that constrained him and could go back to being the man he was meant to be)—but, no tears. How does one cry for the passing on of a man who is not really your father, and whom your father would have hated becoming?

After settling in the kid, and putting the baby to breast, I buckled my seatbelt and was waiting for the plane to take-off, when the stewardess came around with the tray of toffees. My hands automatically reached out for the tray, then pulled back—never again would I pick five toffees from that tray. The dam burst; tears flowed.

Before deplaning, I asked the stewardess for five toffees.

When we journey to the other world, we are not supposed to take anything with us, but as his ashes floated down the river, my father had something clenched in his fists—five airline toffees to sustain him on the Journey.

When I travel, which is now seldom, I always pick up five airline toffees for my kids. Some traditions are worth keeping.

Natasha Ramarathnam

Lessons from Life

I was seventeen years old, studying in the 12th standard in a boarding school and harbouring dreams of becoming a famous doctor. My medical dreams were influenced by the fact that my family comprised plenty of doctors and medical students.

The October holidays were upon us and I couldn't wait to see my parents. I thought I would surprise them by arriving earlier than planned. While sitting in the bus, I went over some questions in English grammar and physics problems that I needed help with, knowing that my father would be ready to guide me. I smiled at that thought. What a wonderful teacher he was! So immersed was I in fantasising about my parents' reaction on seeing me that I was oblivious of the stiff breeze blowing on my face.

My mom opened the door and almost screamed in excitement! Her face clearly told me how much she had been missing me! I asked for my dad only to be told that he had gone to the florist regarding my sister's wedding. He had taken his brand new scooter for the purpose.

I waited for my father eagerly, planning to stand behind the door so that I could pop out and shock him! A bigger shock awaited all of us ...

My patience was wearing thin. Why was he taking so long?

The doorbell finally rang and I quickly got ready behind the door. Mom opened the door, but to my surprise and disappointment it was not my father, but a stranger. I heard him say that the 'saheb' from this house had had an accident and was being taken to the hospital by some passers-by.

Dad had a brain haemorrhage due to the head injury he had sustained, and as a result, was in a coma for several days. The helmet system was still optional those days. He was so careful a rider; how unfair that he had to suffer due to somebody else's fault! The neurologist wasn't too sure of his chances of survival. We prayed desperately as we waited for him to come out of his coma, hoping that after that, everything would be normal again.

By a lucky coincidence, dad's brother, a famous plastic surgeon in the US, happened to visit us the day of the accident. He stayed back with us for more than a month, looking after my father, day in and day out, often skipping meals and hardly ever sleeping. It was as though God had sent my uncle just to save Dad. Observing him that month, I saw just how much he loved and respected his elder brother and what a strong emotional bond they shared.

And then there was my cousin, also a doctor, who worked tirelessly alongside my uncle. My brother, who was a medical intern at that time, was there too.

Finally the day came when Dad woke up, opened his eyes and moved his arms and feet a few inches. After the agonising wait, our joy knew no bounds when he managed to focus his eyes on our faces. We waited for him to smile and call us by our names and talk to us. To our disbelief, he could not recognise any of us, not even my mother! It took him close to a month to identify us. but he had forgotten everything. We waited patiently as he slowly relearned our names; whenever he wanted to call us, he would look up his notebook where he'd had our names written. He had lost the ability to form meaningful sentences and the daily speech therapy sessions hardly helped. And that was not all. At the time of the accident, Dad was the head of the weaving department in a textile industry; but he lost most of the technical knowledge that was necessary for his job. After a few months it became obvious that he had to resign. We packed our bags and moved back to Bangalore, our home town.

The four of us, my brother, my sisters and I, were still studying. Life, as we knew it, had changed drastically for all of us. Dad spent most of his time at home. It took him years to accept the hard fact that he could not work anymore. Mom shouldered the new responsibilities that had been thrust upon her in addition to the ones she already had. It was a painful realisation for us that Dad was no longer the same person we knew. But we never gave up hope that, someday, we would get back the father we knew.

We faced financial hardship for several years. We quickly learnt how to live simply and without any luxuries. We went through innumerable unpleasant and awkward social situations whenever people openly showed their pity.

These factors influenced the kind of person I turned out to be. Though I always got excellent grades in school and was confident of securing a medical seat, I had to take the entrance exam in Coimbatore, where I had been studying. Taking the entrance exam meant that someone in the family would have to accompany me all the way there and back. Also, studying medicine was going to be expensive. At that point in time, the two immediate priorities were looking after my father and fresh arrangements for my sister's wedding. My family was already struggling to make ends meet . . . how could I possibly demand more of them?

So, that meant that I could not fulfil my ambition of becoming a doctor. Though it was a huge disappoint for me, I focused on excelling in college so that I could make a career for myself as quickly as possible. I topped Bangalore University in my subject and thus earned a scholarship for my M.Sc. course. I completed my post-graduation in zoology, once again getting the first rank and thus receiving the gold medal. I started teaching in the same college where I had earned my degree. I declined the research fellowship that I was offered since the stipend amount was less than what my job as a lecturer offered.

All through these years, I missed talking to Dad. I had always discussed academics, my goals and how I'd go about achieving them, with him. Though he was there physically, I could not reach out and connect with him in the same manner as before. Today Dad is eighty-three years old, and spends most of his day trying to read the newspaper and understanding it.

I was always close to my mother too. It was from her that I learnt what it meant to lead a selfless life. She took all the hardships life had thrown her way and concentrated on her duties towards Dad and all of us. What surprises me most is the way my mother looks after him. She is still as patient as ever and in spite of her own deteriorating health, showers him with all the love she can by doing everything within her means to make him comfortable. I can't help but wonder where she got the strength to continue, despite the trauma she must have gone through. She was and is a giver, without any expectations in return. She is my idol; the person I love, respect and admire the most.

It took me decades to come to terms with how life had changed for us. Despite all that we had to go through, none of us let it stop us. We all had our individual goals and persevered to reach them successfully. Our grit and determination to make the most of whatever opportunities we had were only strengthened by the situations we faced and the experiences we gained. Indeed, life's most difficult lessons were also the richest, making winners of us all.

It's true, my dreams of becoming a doctor were dashed, but today, I am not just happy being an educator but also extremely excited about my work; looking for innovations all the time and thinking up ways and means of improving my lessons and making my students smile. The sparkle in their eyes assures me that they enjoy learning, and whenever my old students write to me, or come to meet me and touch my feet, well, these make for the most precious and touching moments in my life.

Sandhya Sitaram

October

The October of 1998 changed my perspective on death; and it bonded us cousins, all twenty-two of us, forever in one memory that is revived in a solemn moment every year.

Grandfather, or Muthachan, was then ninety-eight and we were impatiently waiting for him to hit the century mark. We had celebrated his eighty-fourth birthday last in pomp in true Indian tradition. He was still very active and extremely proud of his brood of grandchildren. We weren't all of us very close, but polarised in interests. Some of us were achievers, some were not; and he was not a saint; he told us to our face if our actions did not please him. You can imagine it was as varied a group as could be with twenty-two different persons.

Muthachan was as well-prepared for death as he had been in life. He had a notebook that recorded absolutely every telephone number that needed to be called when he died, an envelope holding the amount needed for the funeral, and his clothes for the last journey. He wished all formalities connected with death to be over with the cremation. His only regret was: 'So many important people would come here; I won't be able to see any of them!'

In late July he fell, broke his thigh bone and slowly lapsed into a state of coma. I visited him at the hospital on 4 October, and found him almost unresponsive. My ninety-three-year-old grandmother was sitting staidly by his side, quite unaware of what has happening to her husband of seventy-three years. Sudhammavan, his favourite son, was doing most of the nursing. Sudhammavan joked about Muthachan's illness, as was his way; he found an element of satire in everything. Not that we didn't enjoy it; that acid tongue is a genetic gift we all possessed. Jokes apart, though, we knew Muthachan would soon leave us.

I went back to my city and my life. My new landline connection had come through on 6 October and I had made my first call to my grandmother. Within half an hour, the phone had rung in my house, and I had rushed to receive my first call. It was Sudhammavan; he had just talked to his mother. He was actually our window to the world. Sudhammavan was employed with the telephone department and managed to keep in touch with almost all his family regularly. 'So I have another number to call now!' he had said.

That night we had a long power cut. When the telephone bell pealed at two hours past midnight, I was dog-tired, wide awake and fanning the kids with a piece of newspaper. I asked my husband to get the phone. I sensed it was bad news arriving at this odd hour and braced myself to hear about Muthachan. My husband returned, looking solemn and I was almost saying, 'Come on, out with it!' when he said, a little hesitantly: 'It's Sudhammavan, he has had an accident!'

It didn't sink in, so what they say is true: bad news numbs you. I didn't speak for quite a few minutes. I still remember that night, it was hot and stuffy in the room, we couldn't open the windows because of the mosquitoes, and it was eerily still. The telephone rang again and this time it was my cousin, weeping profusely. They hadn't told his mother, and wanted me to do that. 'Wait till it's dawn,' was her advice. I knew it was bad; Sudhammavan was on a ventilator.

We went over to Cochin and at my cousin's house I found the whole family in a state of total collapse. His six sisters were speechless with grief. We, the second generation, were now positioned between grief and concern. Our grandmother had to be told the bad news, Muthachan had to be looked after and Sudhammavan's death was only a formality that awaited a hospital declaration. I went to the hospital with a cousin and was told we could go in to see him inside the intensive care unit; something allowed only if the condition was terminal. The cousin went inside first and came out weeping loudly, 'That is not Sudhammavan, it is someone else.' I had heard that the injury had been on the head, he had been run over; I went back without seeing him, and remembered the last joke he had made, stroking his salt and pepper beard.

On 8 October Sudhammavan was declared dead. He was cremated according to Hindu tradition; fourteen boys of the family bore his body on their shoulders for the last rites and we girls struggled with our own tears and consoled the siblings of the man who left on his last journey. It was the first time that all of us were present together in several years. We came back to my cousin's house immediately, since our grandmother was alone there with an old retainer. She could not face the cremation. Someone made some kanji, rice porridge, and we asked people to eat. None of us had had food for almost twenty-four hours, but the elders still couldn't swallow a morsel.

The band of cousins sat down to eat, but there wasn't any side dish to go with the kanji. My husband went out to a nearby shop and brought in a bottle of garlic pickle; nothing extraordinary, but it would help the food down our throats. In a few minutes, the bottle was half empty; the pickle was proving very tasty and surprisingly lifted our mood. Someone made a feeble joke and all of us tried to listen. Slowly, without realising it, we were all smiling at an incident a cousin was relating. I asked him, 'Who told you this, it's really ridiculous!' And he replied, 'Who else but Sudhammavan!' A moment of silence and we were all jolted back into the present.

This would have been Sudhammavan's favourite moment, sitting among his numerous nephews and nieces and teasing one or other of them. We felt that he was among us that one second. That moment has gone by in time, but stayed in our hearts. We are now spread over the globe, but we share one moment over which we are all sentimental. That has built a rare bond between us.

The October rains now started in real earnest. The days were wet and black in mood ... it was almost like we were waiting for something to happen, perhaps Muthachan's death? He had now been removed to my aunt's house in Kochi. We waited around extending our leave, now in a close web spun by tragedy.

Muthachan followed his son on 18 October, and his last journey was every bit as grand as he wished, and his son had gone on in advance to prepare his bed over there. His notebook of phone numbers was used a second time in two weeks. And the boys of the family repeated a funeral ceremony a second time in a fortnight. The funeral pyre was on the family grounds, and we watched the flames slowly burning Muthachan's frail body into ash, from the window.

October is still a month that brings us memories, tears and nostalgia; and we remember to keep in contact on 8 October more than any other day of the year!

Suneetha B.

The Blue Sweater

I was very excited about going home for the first time after I'd started working and moved to Bangalore. It was time to celebrate Diwali and, incidentally, my birthday. Having never missed celebrating a birthday at home, I was pleased at being able to keep up the tradition even after moving out!

My best friend was also going to be in Nagpur then. She had moved to Pune after we graduated and had taken up a job there. So we were seeing each other after almost four months. As was our habit during college days, we both took off from our respective homes to run some errands together, catching some coffee and snacks on the way. Ultimately, we ended up in Piramyd Mall for coffee. We chatted our hearts out before hitting the women's-wear section. Since it was my birthday, she wanted to buy me something. After ambling through the aisles, we singled out a white Pepe T-shirt. But she thought it would look better with a sweater. So she bought me a blue Provogue sweater.

I took good care of the sweater for the most part; always got it dry-cleaned and used it only for special occasions. Every time I wore it, it would remind me of her and of the good times we had spent together. Of the times when she borrowed my pyjamas when we had a sleepover at my place, and the times when I borrowed hers when we were at hers;

the times we made cold coffee at midnight while she constantly tickled me to annoy me (and succeeded!); when her mom made vanilla ice cream for our night out and she was excited as a child all evening about it, only to end the affair with one spoonful of ice cream before declaring, 'I'm done', while I and our other friend tried our best to finish it (now people know why she is the thinnest among the three of us); the times when we had heart-to-heart chats till three in the morning and others when we made plans to stay up all night but dozed off even before the clock struck one!

We had our differences. There were not many things we did similarly or agreed upon. We didn't have the same hobbies. We had totally different temperaments. Yet, when she was around, I was in my comfort zone. It felt familiar and good. And it was this feeling that made me call her my best friend.

She got married last November. She was the youngest of the three of us and we were surprised that she should be the first one to get married. Being at her wedding was slightly strange—I did not want to let go of her, yet I knew there really was nothing to hold on to . . . just warm thoughts and happy memories.

A few weeks ago, the blue sweater went into the washing machine with my other clothes, and because of some piece of garment, got yellow marks all over it. I was crestfallen at first—it was my favourite sweater, it was a gift, it was a gift from her!

But this past Saturday, I came home soaked to the bone in Bangalore rain and even after I had changed into dry clothes I was feeling quite cold. So I pulled out the blue sweater, as I wouldn't be wearing it outside or on special occasions anymore. It felt so good to be wrapped in that sweater—warm and cosy.

In that moment I realised what a good thing it had been for

that sweater to get stained! Now I could wear it all the time, whenever I was cold, whenever I was feeling lonely, whenever I missed her. As other responsibilities, marriage and work build walls between us and I hardly hear from her; but I have found a way to feel her presence. I have found a bridge to the good times, to the memories, to her. Maybe someday she will walk on the bridge too and we will smile about all this. Till then, I am going to make do with what I have of her: warm thoughts and happy memories—and a blue sweater.

Anupama Kondayya

The Chair

He wouldn't let me use the chair for my experiments in carpentry. 'See this dining table?' he said one day, when I petulantly demanded to know why I shouldn't take the chair apart to learn the fine art of furniture-making. 'It's the finest I could afford. You can saw it to pieces if you like. But don't touch the chair.' My teenage soul rebelled at being forbidden to touch the piece. After all, I wanted to be a master carpenter like my grandpa had been.

I couldn't see what the big deal was. Sure, it was an old chair. A small chair made for a child. I knew the story behind it too. His father, my grandfather, had made several chairs for the local school, and this had been a spare, an extra. I myself had sat in similar chairs in the same school, secretly proud that my grandfather had probably made several of the chairs that accommodated a couple of generations of schoolboys. But it still didn't explain why I couldn't dismantle that chair to learn the secrets of dovetailing and tongue-and-groove joints.

The chair came to represent my teenage arguments with my father as we struggled with issues of leadership, control and independence. He was being unreasonable, my teenage mind screamed, whenever he tried to lay down the law without explaining why, just like he had about the chair.

The years telescoped to my thirtieth. The issue of the chair had been forgotten, as had most of the issues we had fought about when I was a teenager. Against all odds, I had secured a job in Dubai. The night before I left, he sat stroking the chair in a peculiar manner. He would rub his thumb along the edge of the seat, while his thick fingers, the fingers of an artisan, not an artist, caressed the strut that supported the seat. In his usual style, he began speaking with no preamble, 'He liked to stroke it like this. And one night, he called me and told me to take care of Ma, your grandmother, as he stroked the chair. I didn't know why he was telling me that. I didn't know why he was stroking the chair. In the morning, he was gone. He died with his hand on this chair.' He looked at me, and it was the first time in thirty years my father let me see any emotion in him. 'Ma,' he said, blinking back the tears I would see only once in my lifetime, 'told me why he liked to stroke the chair. He was never around to caress us, so he took the chair with him wherever he had to go to make the money to keep us in school.' He paused, then, 'Go to sleep. We have to leave early so you can catch your flight.'

As I boarded the plane a few months later for his funeral, I realised why he wouldn't let me touch the chair, and why he had stroked it the night before I left, as his father had, the night he bid goodbye to his son.

Some answers we get only when we're older.

Deepak Morris

Vini

A shell fell directly into the bunker.

There were six of us taking cover while heavy shelling was on at our location in the remote post on the icy heights of Siachen Glacier. When I recovered from the impact of the explosion of that bomb, I was surprised to find myself alive and unhurt. Everyone else lay dead around me. Strangely, I was numb to any thought at that moment, except for this one: I had not even told her that I loved her!

Amidst the chaos of the days that followed that bombing, I found time to write to her on a torn sheet of paper. No preamble, no flowery language—I even forgot to mention that I thought she was the most beautiful girl I had ever met. I simply wrote that I loved her and wanted her to be my wife.

I was all of twenty-one then, and she was still in college. I was fresh out of the military academy on my first posting in Ladakh. Both our fathers were Army officers serving in the same station and that is how we had met, several years before. She was very bright academically and her parents had high hopes for her career. Disappointing them, she told them that all she wanted to do in life was to be my wife.

That was Vini—who made me the sole focus of her life. The next six years passed in a dizzy blur of love and bliss. We moved often due to my postings. We lived in mud houses called 'bashas' or dreadful married officers' barracks. But those bashas were our palaces and there we made the most amazing memories. There was not much to do for wives in those remote areas, so Vini taught herself to cook the most delectable dishes and mastered desserts. She also gifted me my most precious gift, our daughter Shagun. I felt that I had been given everything by God already, and would not need to ask him for anything more.

Little did I know that I would spend the next twelve years of my life begging God for yet another day—another day that my beloved Vini could live.

When she turned twenty-six, Vini noticed rashes on her skin. Fearing an infection, we visited a dermatologist. His diagnosis shattered our perfect life. Vini had lupus, a rare disease. It is an autoimmune disorder which effects all the organs of the body, gradually killing each in random order. Worse still was the news that lupus was incurable, and to be told that Vini had about two years more to live.

We were young and optimistic and thought of ourselves as invincible. We came from well-heeled, upper-class families, and had access to the medical facilities that the world had to offer. I made it my mission to learn everything that I could find on lupus. I delved into medical research being carried out in any medical facility in the world through the Internet and books. All concurred on one thing: no cure was available. There were several suggestions on how to prolong the patient's time though, and we started working towards that. By then, her disease had spread to her lungs and heart.

Then started the next phase of our life. Acceptance. Once we had accepted that this had happened, we decided that we were not going to allow it to destroy the joy of our remaining days together. We started living life on a quick march. No desire was left unfulfilled; no dream was left without being chased. Every opportunity we got we dined at the best restaurants, saw every movie that Bollywood and Hollywood rolled out. Every weekend involved a picnic to the countryside. We squeezed out the maximum that every day had to offer.

Once, while I was doing a military training course in Pune, she asked me to sell our rickety car and buy an SUV, which was beyond my financial means. But, her wish was mine and we bought a second-hand one. That car earned me the title of 'Raju Guide', as we scoured every place worth visiting within three hundred kilometres of Pune.

We lived our life double-time. The more her condition deteriorated, the more intensely we lived. Our love and devotion for each other grew to obsessive levels. We discussed Vini's illness openly and dealt with her frequent hospital visits in a matter-of-fact way. Our daughter grew up in this environment. The three of us were super company. Vini kept us fully occupied with her plans to live more, do more and see more on an everyday basis.

She pushed me to do my best—not just by living life to the fullest—but also in my career. When I was awarded a prestigious UN assignment in Africa, she urged me take it up as it would do wonders for my career besides giving me invaluable international exposure. Despite her condition, she sacrificed one whole year of togetherness and lived alone in Delhi with our Shagun. On my return, I was promoted to the rank of a colonel and deployed to command my unit at Ahmedabad.

After a year of separation, living together again was even more special. We bought a new car, which gave us fresh wings to travel. We made new friends who loved us for what we had come to stand for—'live life to the fullest, every day'. We partied like never before. We attended every party even though it was becoming increasingly difficult for Vini to climb stairs, live without air-conditioning or be out in the sun.

Diwali 2008 was approaching. Our friends dropped in to invite us to a Diwali party the coming Saturday. True to form, Vini offered to bring the dessert. She lay in bed that day, scarcely lifting her head, but her spirit was bright as ever. Still fussing if somebody saw her in her pyjamas and still planning desserts to make. Our friends did not have a Diwali party that Saturday. For the next day Vini died.

She was thirty-eight years, and eight days old.

She loved me more than any woman could love a man. The best compliment I have ever received I did not receive in person. Her friend told me, after she died, that Vini had once said, 'My skin is turning so bad, I have warts and marks all over me, but Ashu still makes me feel like the most beautiful woman in this world. I want to live a little bit longer only so that I may love him some more.'

Col. Popli
(As told to Vandana Tewari Yadav)

More Chicken Soup?

Share your heart with the rest of the world. If you have a story, poem or article (your own or someone else's) that you feel belongs in a future volume of Chicken Soup for the Indian Soul, please email us at cs.indiansoul@westland-tata.com or send it to:

Westland Ltd
S-35A, 3rd Floor
Green Park Main Market
New Delhi 110 016

We will make sure that you and the author are credited for the contribution. Thank you!

Contributors

Alaka Yeravadekar is a writer, trainer and cost-consultant. A keen birdwatcher with a passion for music, her travel writing, photographs, and poetry have been published by various print and online magazines. She can be reached at alakaa@gmail.com.

Ameet Kumar Surana has a special child, Darshan, with a genetic disorder (MPS 2), and a normal child, Hrithik. Darshan has made him realise that it is important to live every moment of life and to live in the present. He lives in a quaint little city called Coimbatore, Tamil Nadu, and he can be reached at ameets06@yahoo.com.

Amita Dalal is a sitar player attached with the Saptak school of music. A regular on AIR and television, she has performed in Japan, Russia and Germany. A graduate in B.A, L.L.B, she is also involved in hand-block printing on fabrics. She can be reached at amberishdalal@hotmail.com.

Amreeta Sen is a full-time mother and a part-time writer. She has worked at the *Statesman* for many years before deciding to quit and enjoy her life with her daughter and son at home. She still writes for the *Statesman*, *Times of India* and *Tribune*, Chandigarh. Her published books are *Kurukshetra*, *Kaikeyi* and *The Lost Unicorn*. Her fourth, 'Kanya and Other Tales', is due to be published next year.

Anil Agarwal is director, Kashiram Textile Mills. This is his first venture into the field of writing. He is interested in photography, general knowledge, travelling, meeting people and watching Discovery and English movies. He also takes care of his family-run charitable ayurvedic clinic. He can be reached at anil1sin@gmail.com.

Writing for the last three decades, **Anjana Jha** has been published by major newspapers and magazines including *Statesman*, *Times of India*, *Hindustan Times*, *Eve's Weekly*, *Femina* and *Woman's Era*. Besides writing fiction, human interest, travel articles and profiles, she has edited a number of books and publications. Currently based in Delhi, she works for *Harmony—Celebrate Age*, a magazine for senior citizens. She can be reached at anjanajha04@yahoo.com.

Ankur Garg is a software engineer and has worked with Infosys for two years. Currently, he's pursuing his MBA from NMIMS, Mumbai. He has been writing short-stories, poems and vignettes for the last five years. Most of his creations are inspired by real-life experiences. He can be reached at ankur26garg@gmail.com.

Anu Chopra is an Ahmedabad-based writer. She has published a book of short stories called *Scattered Thoughts*. She loves reading, especially women-centric Indian fiction. She can be reached at anuchopra77@gmail.com.

Anupama Kondayya is an analyst by profession and a traveller, photographer, musician and book-lover by passion. But she is a writer above all, as writing helps her express all that she experiences while engaging in either her profession or her passions. She also freelances as a writer. She is based in Bangalore and can be reached at anupamakondayya@gmail.com.

Arijit Ghosh is a full-time dad, ruing the fact that his son is growing up faster than he imagined, gradually making his job as dad redundant. He has dreamt of being an actor, a writer, a bodybuilder, rally-driver, and cross-dresser but couldn't make up his mind about any particular passion. He can be reached at arijitchief@gmail.com, an email account he seldom checks.

Avantika Debnath, also known as Avni, is a simple girl. Like anyone else, she cries and laughs, but one thing that makes her different is that she makes a story out of every drop of tear she sheds and every ring of her laughter. Avni is blessed with the ability to hope, and her hope is that people around the world will come together spreading joy and goodwill for everyone in God's creation. She can be reached at avantika.debnath@gmail.com.

When not struggling with her first-born's homework or at attempts to turn her second-born bilingual, **Baisali Chatterjee Dutt** harbours illusions of being a writer. She still clutches a tattered notebook full of angsty poems she wrote another lifetime ago, close to her heart, along with several other half-written manuscripts, waiting for a benevolent publisher. She has an MA in French, but her time is spent in trying to master the '1001 Ways to Keep Your Child Occupied on Rainy Days and Holidays'. She can be reached at baisali.cd@gmail.com.

L.K. Baweja retired as general manager. As a hobby, he writes short stories on personal experiences that have been published in *Reader's Digest*, *Dignity Dialogue* and *Harmony*.

Beryl Kunjavu is a software engineer who lives in Mumbai. She loves to travel, read and write about her experiences. Her articles have appeared in the *Times of India*, various portals and newsletters. She can be reached at beryl_kun@yahoo.com.

Bhagyashree Sowani stays in Ahmedabad. She likes to travel. She hopes to someday visit every country in the world, and also to sample every cuisine. Her email address is bsowani@gmail.com.

Chitra Vashisht is a reiki grandmaster and a tarot reader. She teaches yoga and meditation to underprivileged women. She is also associated with Caring Hand for Children, a US-based NGO looking after the education of 1,000 children in India.

Christina Daniels is a communications professional, with a diverse background that brings together exposure to training, new media, e-learning, print journalism, corporate communication, developmental communication and research. She has authored the novel *Ginger Soda Lemon Pop* and holds a Master's in New Media from the

London School of Economics and Political Science. She can be reached at christinadaniels22@yahoo.com.

Deepak Morris is an author, playwright, stage director, stage actor and drama consultant based in Pune. He has authored several guidebooks on managerial subjects and has written over a dozen plays, skits, monologues and short scenes. His plays have been staged in several countries across the world, including the US and Canada. He can be reached at deepakmorris@rhapsodytheatre.org.

Dhruv Katoch is an alumnus of Sherwood College, Nainital and the National Defence Academy. A third generation Army officer, he retired as a major-general from the Indian Army. He writes regularly on security and defence-related issues and on matters of societal and environmental concern. He can be reached at dhruvkatoch@hotmail.com and at his blog, dhruvkatoch.blogspot.com.

Dimple Ranpara is a budding civil engineering student born and brought up in the Steel City of the Tatas. She is known for her leadership qualities and her creative goof-ups. She believes not in being different but doing simple things differently.

Dipika Mukherjee's debut novel 'Thunder Demons' was long-listed for the Man Asian Literary Prize 2009 and she won the Platform Flash Fiction competition in April 2009. In the past year, her work has appeared in the *Asia Literary Review*, *The South Asia Review*, *Flashquake*, *Freefall*, *Pilot Pocket Book 5*, *Quarterly Literary Review of Singapore*, *New Writing Dundee* and *Muse India*. Her first poetry collection, *The Palimpsest of Exile*, was published by Rubicon Press (Canada) in April 2009. She currently lives in Shanghai, China.

Divyaa Kummar is a spiritual facilitator in Mumbai, reaching out to many through her weekly discourses, writings, meditation groups, personal energy and tarot sessions. She can be reached at www.divyaakummar.com.

Gunit Locham is an eighth grade student at Sacred Heart, Church Park, Chennai. She is a voracious reader and has written this article in fond memory of her beloved grandfather, who is also her role model. She can be reached at nix710@gmail.com.

H.P. Singh is an IPS officer of the Gujarat cadre. He can be reached at singh.hp@hotmail.com.

Heartcrossings is a recent immigrant to the States, single mother, passionate about motherhood, reading, mashing up recipes from around the world, good music and cinema and blogging. Her day job is IT consulting and she often writes about her perspectives on technology and the industry. If she could have a genie grant her three wishes, they would be: 1) Live in a different country every year 2) Be her daughter's best friend always 3) Die early one morning in Spring surrounded by grandchildren, mountains and ocean. She blogs at heartcrossings.blogspot.com

Heena Patel is an environmental engineer-turned-classical musician from Canada, currently living in India. She is training to become a classical tabla player under Pandit Divyang Vakil and working for the preservation and promotion of Indian classical music. She blogs at rhythmicthoughts.wordpress.com and can be reached at heena.tabla@gmail.com.

Huta Raval, a topper in English literature and journalism, is a strong believer in the karma philosophy ('As you sow, so shall you reap'). After an eleven-year stint in the corporate world, she is currently engaged in guiding students towards a better academic career. To connect and exchange your views, mail her at hutaraval@gmail.com.

Born in Edinburgh in 1944, **Jane Bhandari** has lived in India for over forty years and is a writer and occasional painter. She co-ordinates 'Loquations', a Mumbai poetry reading group, and has authored two volumes of poetry, *Single Bed* and *Aquarius*. She has also written two collections of short stories for children, *The Round Square Chapatti* and *The Long Thin Jungle*. A third collection of poems and a novel are in progress.

Janki Vasant is the founder trustee of Samvedana, a registered trust working for underprivileged slum children in India, with a focus on education and other welfare activities. Its vision is to touch the lives of economically-challenged children with a focus on their overall development using education as a tool for grooming a balanced personality, thus working towards a literate India. Her email id is janki@samvedana.org.in.

Kabir Singh Bhandari currently works in the *Hindustan Times* in Kolkata. He is active in the theatre scene in the city. He can be reached at kabirscorpio@gmail.com.

Komal Venkataraman is a business development manager in a large organisation in Chennai. He loves to read and write, has special interest in religion and temple history, and plays cricket and badminton. He can be reached at komalvenki@yahoo.com.

Lakshmi Madhusoodanan is an English teacher who has taught English in different parts of India to school children from the ages of five to eighteen. Writing is, for her, an outlet for creativity, a need of her profession as well as a stress-buster. She can be reached at lakshmi@teacher.com.

Mahendra Waghela is an artist/writer. You can reach him at waghela.mahendra@gmail.com.

Mahesh Dattani is a playwright, stage director and filmmaker. In 1998, he received the Sahitya Akademi Award for his collection of plays. Dattani's current home is in the city of Mumbai. He may be contacted at mahesh.dattani@gmail.com or Facebook.

Malavika Thiagaraja writes poetry and short stories as a hobby. Her works are available on her blog at tmalavika.blogspot.com. She can be reached at tmalavika@gmail.com.

Atmapreeta / Manjushree Abhinav is a filmmaker who wrote a novel, *A Grasshopper's Pilgrimage*, then became a primary school teacher.

Max Babi is a science writer, extensively published on the web, is a multi-lingual thinker passionate about music and poetry. He lives and works at Pune. He can be reached at maxbabi@gmail.com or through www.maxbabi.com.

Dr Meenakshi Roy is a graduate of the Armed Forces Medical College, Pune. After having served the Indian Army Medical Corps for six years, she voluntarily resigned from service in 2007 as a major in the Army and moved to the US to settle down with her husband. She is currently studying as well as pursuing her interests in fiction writing. She also blogs at mishyroy.blogspot.com. She can be contacted at mishyroy@gmail.com.

S. Meera is a work-from-home-mother of two. She loves to read in her spare time. Though writing is her profession, she also spends some time writing for her own pleasure. She is also passionate about her dance, and gives group and solo bharatnatyam performances. She can be reached at meerasampath@hotmail.com.

Mita Banerjee is a wife, mother and a published writer. She has been pursuing her twin passions of teaching and writing for more than three decades, even as she accompanied her Air Force husband on postings to remote corners of the country. She was honoured with a Lifetime Achievement Award for highlighting numerous issues regarding the environment, women, children and social welfare. She can be contacted at mitabaner@gmail.com.

Monika Pant is a teacher at La Martiniere Girls' College, Lucknow, teaching English to senior students. She is interested in writing on all subjects, particularly about relationships, perspectives and points of view, experiences that open one's mind to realities and about big and small issues of life. She has written a novel based on these experiences and is looking for a publisher who would publish this novel. She can be reached at mpant65@gmail.com.

Ever since **Monisha Sen** accepted that being a mother all day and night was boring and not good for the kids, she started working. Since she couldn't go back to her previous, demanding job, she now works from home as a trends analyst (for money) and a writer (for fun). She is in Mumbai, and can be contacted at sen.monisha@gmail.com.

Namratha Kumar is a freelance writer staying in Bandra, Mumbai. She roots for the underdog and is currently working on a children's fantasy novel. She can be reached at namratha2006@yahoo.co.in.

Natasha Ramarathnam is a graduate of the Indian Institute of Management-Ahmedabad, who worked in an investment bank for over six years before moving to the non-profit sector. She lives in Mumbai with her husband, two sons and an ever-increasing collection of books. When she is not answering questions thrown at her by her kids, Natasha tries to make time for running, gardening and photography. She can be reached at natasha@magicbusindia.org.

Neelam Kothari is a jeweller and enjoys her romance with gems and stones. She can be reached at nkothari_64@yahoo.co.in.

Nikhil Anil Kulkarni is pursuing his third year BBA in MIT college in Pune. He has a firm belief that 'humanity is the best religion in this world'. Writing thoughtful as well as comedic stories is his hobby. He can be reached at nikhil2812@gmail.com.

Nipun Mehta is the founder of CharityFocus, which leverages technology to create ripples of goodness in the world. In 2003, they printed 100 'Smile Cards' to encourage small acts of kindness, and today, that experiment has spread to millions worldwide. Read more about it at www.helpothers.org.

Pesi Jal Padshah is a retired senior citizen who used to be a physical training instructor. He loves motorbikes, animals and children. Among other institutions, he taught at West Wind, a kindergarten school in Mumbai, for thirty-five years, until he retired in 1997. Since then he has been leading a quiet life in Pune, except for still risking his neck on a motorbike. He can be reached at 020-40046331.

Piyush Panwar was born in Khandwa in 1959. He is a geologist with an oil and gas consulting firm. He did his Master's in geology from Punjab University, Chandigarh before joining ONGC where he worked for over two decades living in different parts of the country. He is very fond of reading and travelling and maintains a travelogue that he plans to publish one day. He currently lives with his wife and two sons in Kuala Lumpur, Malaysia.

Priya Pathiyan, currently editor of *Mother & Baby*, India's premier parenting magazine, has been a lifestyle journalist with the mainstream media for twelve years. She has also co-authored India's first comprehensive wedding guide, *Wedding Belles*. She has travelled extensively, loves movies, music and dancing and is trying out different cuisines. She is passionate about reading, wildlife and animal welfare, Mumbai history, fragrances and a lot of other things! She can be reached at priya.pathiyan@gmail.com.

Puja Madan is a new media consultant and speaker by profession and blogs about her work regularly. She enjoys dabbling in story writing and photography when she gets a chance. You can find out more by visiting www.sulmoz.com.

Raamesh Gowri Raghavan is a poet and writer by night, and a copywriter by day. He lives in Thane near Mumbai and is considered funny company by his friends (at times). He may be reached at azhvan@yahoo.co.in, at the correspondent's risk.

Ramendra Kumar is an award-winning writer for children with fourteen books in English to his credit. His work has been published and reviewed in major newspapers and magazines and translated into several Indian languages as well as Japanese, Spanish, Basque, Sinhala and Mongolian. He is also an inspirational and motivational speaker for children. He can be reached at 25ramendra@gmail.com / 09778401628. To know more about him you can visit his website www.ramendra.com.

Rana Siddiqui Zaman has been a journalist for fourteen years. She lives in Delhi and works with a reputed English newspaper (the *Hindu*). She also curates art shows and appears on television channels as a film and art critic and writes art catalogues.

Rayna Talwar is a people-watcher and aspiring writer. A scientist by training, she is passionate about social causes, ranging from education to poverty alleviation. She lives in Mumbai with her ever-growing collection of books and plants. She can be reached at raynatalwar@gmail.com.

Rehana Ali is a teacher of life sciences and biotechnology at La Martiniere Girls' College, Lucknow. She also heads the school's nature club and works with her students to address environment issues. Most of her stories are based on her experiences as a school teacher, a role she has enjoyed playing for the last thirty years. She can be reached at ali.rehana@gmail.com.

Revathi Seshadri lives in Nagpur with her husband and a few cats and a dog. She writes newspaper middles and is an active member of a few online writers' clubs. She has two daughters, and is a voracious reader; her main interest is books on the subject of the paranormal. Her email id is revathi.seshadri@gmail.com.

Ruma Purkayastha is a psychology major who believes that the human spirit is indomitable. Currently the principal of Navy Children's School, Delhi, Ruma was a teacher for twenty years, a weekly columnist for the *Deccan Chronicle*, Vizag, and hosted a few educational shows on AIR. Passionate about education, her dream is to facilitate a progressive learning system in India.

Sandhya Krishnan is an ex-management consultant and the founder-director of Blue Mango, a multi-ethnic theatre group based in Pittsburgh. Besides acting and reading, she enjoys writing fiction and has several published articles and short stories to her credit. Sandhya is an alumnus of BITS, Pilani and XLRI, Jamshedpur and currently lives with her husband in the US. She can be reached at sandhyakrishnan@gmail.com.

Sangeetha Narayan is a freelance writer based in Ellicott City, Maryland. She completed her Master's in commerce and then moved on to complete a children's literature course from an institute based in Connecticut. A few of her short stories for children have been published in various magazines in India. She also published a short story in *Women's Era*. She can be reached at sursangeet_2000@yahoo.com.

Sangeetha Parthasarathy is a published short fiction writer. She lives and works in New York, and is a consultant by profession. Her hobbies include performing Indian classical music in the US, writing, blogging and travelling. She hopes to publish her first novel soon. She can be reached at salaisangeetha@gmail.com.

Sandhya Sitaram is the director of Zeal Education, an organisation that offers workshops for children and adults. She is a teacher trainer in schools that want a change in the way education is imparted. She is also a consultant corporate (behavioural) trainer for Bharti Airtel. She can be contacted by email at sandhya.sitaram@gmail.com.

Shabbir Merchant is a leadership development consultant and an executive coach in Asia. He is based in Bangalore and consults several Fortune 500 and ET 500 companies in Asia. After more than seventeen years in the corporate world, he discovered his calling was to work with leaders to help them create value for their stakeholders, which led him to start his own firm Valulead Consulting. He can be reached at shabbir@valulead.in.

Shankar Hemmady is a San Francisco-based author, entrepreneur and technologist exploring meaning in all aspects of life. He can be reached on Facebook or LinkedIn.

Shashi Agarwal is a B.Com graduate from Sydenham College of Commerce and Economics. She is a homemaker and has two grown-up daughters. She has always been interested in writing, and writes poems and short stories sporadically. She can be reached at agarwalsash@gmail.com.

Sheetal Goel is an independent marketing and advertising professional, living in a beautiful, green corner in Bandra, Mumbai. She can be reached at sheetal.goel@gmail.com.

Shivana Naidoo resides in Queens, New York. She is South Asian Indo-Caribbean American. Her first time in India was during the Indicorps Fellowship (www.indicorps.org). She is passionate about music, creativity and communication. She is completing her MD and aspires to become a psychiatrist. She can be reached at shivana_naidoo@yahoo.com.

Shriyaa Trivedi is a psychology major student and a budding artist who also likes to write as a mode of expression. Find out more about her at http://aurecca.blogspot.com/ and http://aurecca.deviantart.com/ or reach her at cool.dudette89@gmail.com.

Smriti Lamech is a writer who lives in and loves Delhi. She also loves her babies, her husband and her life, hot chocolate fudge and reading, in no particular order. She loves dabbling and gardening and on a good day fits thirty-six hours into the given twenty-four. On a bad day, she recommends staying out of her way and corresponding via email to smritilamech@gmail.com.

Sreelata Menon is a freelance writer who enjoys writing on all kinds of topics. She writes on current happenings with quite unfailing regularity online as well as for national and international print publications. She also posts weekly blogs on freelance writing and has published many articles on how to go about it. Her book *Freelance Writing for the Newbie Writer* has just been released to some rave reviews. She can be reached at sreelata0@yahoo.co.in.

Sudesna Ghosh is a freelance writer based in Kolkata. She loves writing and spends her spare time working with an NGO for stray dogs. She can be reached at sudesna.ghosh@gmail.com.

Suneetha B. is a freelance writer, journalist and translator who writes in English and Malayalam. She lives in Trivandrum and is also a trainer for creative writing and communication skills. She can be reached at yashovathi@gmail.com.

Sunil Handa (BE-BITS, Pilani, MBA-IIM, Ahmedabad) is an established and respected entrepreneur in the packaging and pharmaceutical industries. He has been a visiting professor at IIM, Ahmedabad for seventeen years, where he offers a course called LEM (Laboratory in Entrepreneurial Motivation). He founded the Eklavya School in Ahmedabad.

Suparnaa Chadda is a media professional who has dabbled with radio and television and the print media. Her most passionate venture till date is the independent documentary, *When Atlas Shrugged—Again,* on the victims of the 2005 Kashmir earthquake. Suparnaa is a single mother of two, an eleven-year-old daughter and a three-year-old mutt adopted from an animal shelter. She can be reached at suparnaas@yahoo.com.

Upreet Dhaliwal is an avid reader of romantic fiction; however, given her hectic lifestyle, which includes patient care, parenting, and house-holding, she can rarely be self-indulgent. Blogging is a recent passion and she can be found on Sulekha.com, where she uses the nom-de-keyboard 'Seeingeye'. She can be reached at upreetdhaliwal@yahoo.com.

Vandana Tewari Yadav was born in a Hindu Brahmin family, did her schooling at Christian convent schools and her graduation in mathematics at Aligarh Muslim University. She works as an air hostess with Air India International. She is a mother of two and married to an Army officer who loves her nomadic lifestyle, which lets her live in various parts of the country and travel around the world.

Vijayalakshmi Ramachandran is the founder president of Roshni, an organisation for the promotion of eye donation and corneal transplantation at Jamshedpur. At present settled in Chennai with her husband, she is also a reiki master and teaches reiki at home and gives healing. She enjoys teaching maths, writing freelance in Tamil and English, reading books and gardening. She can be reached at vijayaramach@gmail.com.

Vrunda Thakkar is a B.Sc LLB. She believes that life is beautiful and full of love. She is an astrologer as well as a tarot card reader.

Permissions

Dear M. Reprinted by permission of Meenakshi Roy. © 2009 Meenakshi Roy.

Dowry. Reprinted by permission of Ramendra Kumar. © 2009 Ramendra Kumar.

Forgiveness. Reprinted by permission of Mahesh Dattani. © 2009 Mahesh Dattani.

His Bumper Sticker Reads, 'Princess on Board'. Reprinted by permission of Monisha Sen. © 2009 Monisha Sen.

How Will You Know When It Is for Real? Upreet Dhaliwal. © 2009 Upreet Dhaliwal.

If Mom Had Been Around. Reprinted by permission of Anusha Parthasarathy. © 2009 Anusha Parthasarathy.

Meeting Kamla. Reprinted by permission of Sangeetha Parthasarthy. © 2009 Sangeetha Parthasarthy.

Not So Ordinary. Reprinted by permission of Nikhil Kulkarni. © 2009 Nikhil Kulkarni.

Overcoming an Addiction. Reprinted by permission of Huta Raval. © 2009 Huta Raval.

Power. Reprinted by permission of Malavika Thiagaraja. © 2009 Malavika Thiagaraja.

The Art of Admonition. Reprinted by permission of Pesi Padshah. © 2009 Pesi Padshah.

The Captain and I. Reprinted by permission of Mahendra Waghela. © 2009 Mahendra Waghela.

The Cheesy Romance That Wasn't. Reprinted by permission of Rayna Talwar. © 2009 Rayna Talwar.

The Cheque. Reprinted by permission of Sheetal Goel. © 2009 Sheetal Goel.

The Divinity of Unconditional Love. Reprinted by permission of Shriyaa Trivedi. © 2009 Shriyaa Trivedi.

The Poker Room. Reprinted by permission of Shashi Agarwal. © 2009 Shashi Agarwal.

The Wisdom Tooth. Reprinted by permission of Puja Madan. © 2009 Puja Madan.

United. Reprinted by permission of Sudesna Ghosh. © 2009 Sudesna Ghosh.

Writing for Chicken Soup. Reprinted by permission of Seema Agarwal. © 2009 Seema Agarwal.

A Different Plane. Reprinted by permission of S. Meera. © 2009 S. Meera.

Fighting Myself. Reprinted by permission of Kabir Singh Bhandari. © 2009 Kabir Singh Bhandari.

Following My Footsteps. Reprinted by permission of Sayli Deshmukh. © 2009 Sayli Deshmukh.

Going to the Roots. Reprinted by permission of Amita Dalal. © 2009 Amita Dalal.

Just a Little Patience. Reprinted by permission of Rayna Talwar. © 2009 Rayna Talwar.

Lessons from a Parking Lot Attendant. Komal Venkataraman. © 2009 Komal Venkatraman

Losing the Battle to Win the War. Reprinted by permission of Christina Daniels. © 2009 Christina Daniels.

My Recollections of Mountaineering. Reprinted by permission of Gunit Locham. © 2009 Gunit Locham.

Sight Beyond Vision. Reprinted by permission of Piyush Panwar. © 2009 Piyush Panwar.

The Edge. Reprinted by permission of Alaka Yeravadekar. © 2009 Alaka Yeravadekar.

The Indomitable Soldier. Reprinted by permission of Mita Banerjee. © 2009 Mita Banerjee.

The Moment You Wish . . . Reprinted by permission of Amita Dalal. © 2009 Amita Dalal.

The Next Best Thing. Reprinted by permission of Suparnaa Chadda. © 2009 Suparnaa Chadda.

A Glimmer of Hope. Reprinted by permission of Shabbir Merchant. © 2009 Shabbir Merchant.

A Hundred and Twenty-Five Rupees. Reprinted by permission of H.P. Singh. © 2009 H.P. Singh.

Be a Troubleshooter. Reprinted by permission of Sunil Handa. © 2009 Sunil Handa.

The Deal . Reprinted by permission of Sunil Handa. © 2009 Sunil Handa.

My Little Step. Reprinted by permission of Heena Patel. © 2009 Heena Patel.

One Life. Reprinted by permission of Dimple Ranpara. © 2009 Dimple Ranpara.

The Finger Bowl. Reprinted by permission of Sreelata Menon. © 2009 Sreelata Menon.

The King of Kings. Reprinted by permission of Bhagyashree Sowani. © 2009 Bhagyashree Sowani.

The Principles of Justice and Humanity. Reprinted by permission of Vrunda Thakkar. © 2009 Vrunda Thakkar.

True Greatness. Reprinted by permission of Rayna Talwar. © 2009 Rayna Talwar.

Working for People. Reprinted by permission of Lakshmi Madhusoodanan. © 2009 Lakshmi Madhusoodanan.

A Messiah in Malaysia. Reprinted by permission of Dipika Mukherjee. © 2009 Dipika Mukherjee.

A Second Chance. Reprinted by permission of Suparnaa Chadda. © 2009 Suparnaa Chadda.

A Second Innings. Reprinted by permission of Anu Chopra. © 2009 Anu Chopra.

Fine Line. Reprinted by permission of Heartcrossings. © 2009 Heartcrossings.

One Rainy Day in Mumbai . Reprinted by permission of Sandhya Krishnan. © 2009 Sandhya Krishnan.

Requiem for Love. Reprinted by permission of Dhruv Katoch. © 2009 Dhruv Katoch.

Science Versus Spirituality. Reprinted by permission of Suparnaa Chadda. © 2009 Suparnaa Chadda.

Someone. Reprinted by permission of Amreeta Sen. © 2009 Amreeta Sen.

Superannuation. Reprinted by permission of Chitra Vashisht. © 2009 Chitra Vashisht.

Tarot. Reprinted by permission of Divyaa Kummar. © 2009 Divyaa Kummar.

The Clear Voice. Reprinted by permission of Janki Vasant. © 2009 Janki Vasant.

The Open Ground of Middle Age. Reprinted by permission of Jane Bhandari. © 2009 Jane Bhandari.

The White Hair. Reprinted by permission of Ankur Garg. © 2009 Ankur Garg.

When My Heart Gave Up. Reprinted by permission of Sangeetha Narayan. © 2009 Sangeetha Narayan.

A Little Love to Spare. Reprinted by permission of Anjana Jha. © 2009 Anjana Jha.

Angels Don't Always Have Wings. Reprinted by permission of Max Babi. © 2009 Max Babi.

Assignment. Reprinted by permission of Avantika Debnath. © 2009 Avantika Debnath.

Blood Donation. Reprinted by permission of Rehana Ali. © 2009 Rehana Ali.

Clapping for God. Reprinted by permission of Beryl Kunjavu. © 2009 Beryl Kunjavu.

For the Tsunami. Reprinted by permission of Manjushree Abhinav. © 2009 Manjushree Abhinav.

Forgotten Names. Reprinted by permission of Arijit Ghosh. © 2009 Arijit Ghosh.

From a Teacher's Desk. Reprinted by permission of Rehana Ali. © 2009 Rehana Ali.

Moment of Clarity. Reprinted by permission of Manjushree Abhinav. © 2009 Manjushree Abhinav.

Music of a Stolen Symphony. Reprinted by permission of Nipun Mehta. © 2009 Nipun Mehta.

Reach Out and Help Someone. Reprinted by permission of Ruma Purkayashta. © 2009 Ruma Purkayastha.

Small Things with Great Love. Reprinted by permission of L.K. Baweja. © 2009 L.K. Baweja.

The Gift of Sight. Reprinted by permission of Vijayalakshmi Ramachandran. © 2009 Vijayalakshmi Ramachandran.

PERMISSIONS

The Scooty Ride. Reprinted by permission of Rana Siddiqui Zaman. © 2009 Rana Siddiqui Zaman.

The Volunteer. Reprinted by permission of Priya Pathiyan. © 2009 Priya Pathiyan.

Vocal in Times of Beauty. Reprinted by permission of Pavi Mehta. © 2009 Pavi Mehta.

A Carnation by Any Other Name. Reprinted by permission of Namratha Kumar. © 2009 Namratha Kumar.

Appu. Reprinted by permission of Revathi Seshadri. © 2009 Revathi Seshadri.

It Happens Only in India. Reprinted by permission of S. Meera. © 2009 S. Meera.

Lost in London. Reprinted by permission of Ameet Surana. © 2009 Ameet Surana.

My Hero. Reprinted by permission of Rehana Ali. © 2009 Rehana Ali.

Of Dal-Chawal and Biryani. Reprinted by permission of Akanksha. © 2009 Akanksha.

On the Birth of My Nephew. Reprinted by permission of Raamesh Gowri Raghavan. © 2009 Raamesh Gowri Raghavan.

Still Indian After Two Hundred Years, Two Oceans, Three Continents and Thousands of Miles of Separation. Reprinted by permission of Shivana Naidoo. © 2009 Shivana Naidoo.

The Green Salwar Kameez, Bindi and Bangles. Reprinted by permission of Janki Vasant. © 2009 Janki Vasant.

The Oil Canvas. Reprinted by permission of Neelam Kothari. © 2009 Neelam Kothari.

Underestimating John. Reprinted by permission of Anu Chopra. © 2009 Anu Chopra.

Wrong Side of Thirty-Five!. Reprinted by permission of Suparnaa Chadda. © 2009 Suparnaa Chadda.

Daddy Comes Home. Reprinted by permission of Shankar Hemmady. © 2009 Shankar Hemmady.

Fighting for Karuna's Dignity. Reprinted by permission of Rehana Ali. © 2009 Rehana Ali.

Five Airline Toffees. Reprinted by permission of Natasha Ramarathnam. © 2009 Natasha Ramarathnam.

Lessons from Life. Reprinted by permission of Sandhya Sitaram. © 2009 Sandhya Sitaram.

October. Reprinted by permission of Suneetha B. © 2009 Suneetha B.

The Blue Sweater. Reprinted by permission of Anupama Kondayya. © 2009 Anupama Kondayya.

The Chair. Reprinted by permission of Deepak Morris. © 2009 Deepak Morris.

Vini. Reprinted by permission of Vandana Tewari Yadav. © 2009 Vandana Tewari Yadav.